D0939790

NUTRITIOUS
& DELICIOUS™

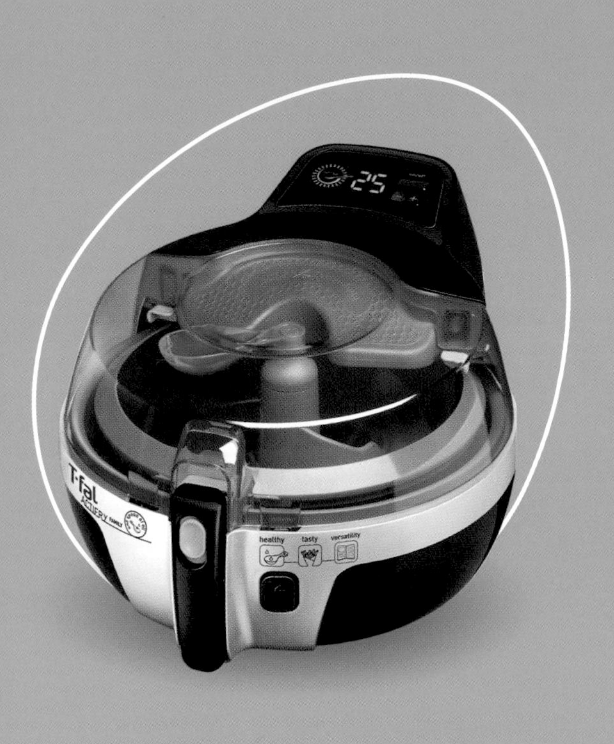
25
T-fal
ACTIFRY
FAMILY
healthy
tasty
versatility

We All Cook!

T-fal®

Contents

T-Fal: Nutritious

Innovating for your health

Nutrition is, of course, about eating a varied and well-balanced diet. But it is not only that, because nutrition is more than the sum of ingredients. How you cook plays a key role in how nutritional value and organoleptic qualities (taste, texture, etc.) are transformed.

And because not all kitchen equipment the same, T-Fal has developed a product line dedicated to ENJOYING NUTRITION MORE: these ingenious appliances preserve nutritional integrity and bring out the real taste of ingredients.

Providing unique solutions

T-fal invests in research to create appliances that have unique nutritional performance, supported by scientific studies.

Sharing information

T-fal has always been a special food partner helping you prepare your meals quickly, practically and easily.

Day after day, T-Fal 's Nutritious & Delicious range helps you share culinary pleasure and a balanced diet by:

- enhancing and preserving the qualities of natural ingredients that are essential to your diet
- limiting the use of fat
- promoting a return to forgotten tastes and ingredients
- limiting the time spent on preparing meals.

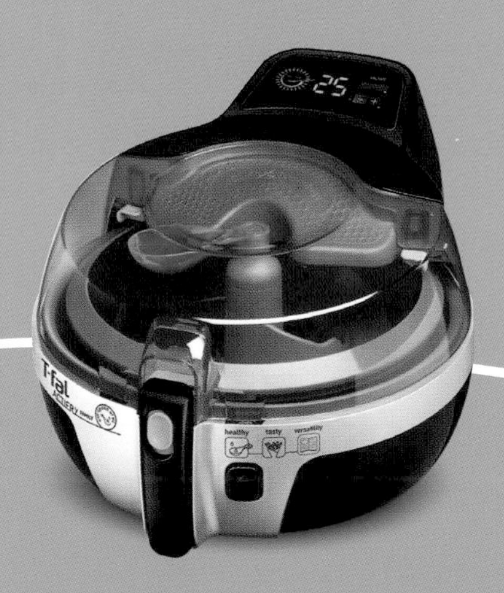

& Delicious Cooking

The story of

ActiFry by Groupe SEB*

T-fal is part of Groupe SEB, world leader in small domestic appliances.

The Groupe SEB (Société d'Emboutissage de Bourgogne) has 150 years of history based on constantly innovating and conquering new markets. SEB's goal is to make life easier for people around the world, providing them with products and new solutions that bring enjoyment and well being.

This mix of inventiveness, ambition and persistence, along with the attention we pay to consumers, has made our group world leader in small household appliances.

Our company headquarters have been located in Burgundy, France, since we were founded, and we have always been inspired by this famous region's historical values, with its recognized gastronomy and unique cultural heritage strongly influenced by the lifestyle of its inhabitants. So, it comes as no surprise that this region is the birthplace of a revolutionary way of cooking!

Today, in addition to simplifying your daily life, we also provide you with delicious culinarymoments and many other agreeable experiences, thanks to products that are perfectly adapted to healthy, flavourful cooking.

ActiFry, Burgundy style

The idea of making homemade fries with very little oil arose a long time ago, and we were able to approach the question from another angle through our research with French universities that focused on the cooking process.

This new knowledge led us to understand the precise role oil plays in cooking and the exact parameters needed to get a crispy outside and a soft inside.

Once we developed and mastered this process, we needed to transpose it in a household appliance. It took no fewer than five generations of prototypes and multiple organoleptic tests to come up with the sought-after quality and results.

Our research and studies led to four different patents concerning this revolutionary procedure. There were more than ten years of research between the initial idea and the first production series in January 2007. Now, as a result of this teamwork, ActiFry is produced by the thousands every day, in France, in the heart of Burgundy.

* T-Fal is part of Groupe SEB, world leader in small household appliances.

ActiFry

ActiFry Revolutionary ActiFry

ActiFry makes 3 lbs (1.5 kg) of real homemade fries, crispy on the outside and soft inside, with only one spoonful of oil! That is less than 3% fat and fries that taste just like those our grandmothers made. With ActiFry, we can use good quality oils that are good for us, so we can vary dishes and flavours. It is part of our Nutritious & Delicious range that combines the latest technology with T-fal's know-how for delicious healthy eating.

ActiFry for the whole family

ActiFry has travelled a lot and people just keep talking about it. ActiFry has won over more than two million consumers around the world, by adapting to their wants and needs, to better satisfy their taste buds. Its cooking talent is without contest and in this book, users will discover healthy recipes, adapted to all ages and to the tastes of everyone in the family: fun and yummy recipes for kids, easy and tasty recipes for teens, and practical, delicious recipes for the entire family together.

Health is important to everyone, which is why around the world, families in-the-know turn to ActiFry, which marries nutritional qualities, good taste and practicality.

ActiFry and the media

Today, not only customers, but also journalists from around the world visit ActiFry's birthplace in the French city of Is-sur-Tille. They want to understand what magic potion gave rise to such innovation. ActiFry even has paparazzi shooting it non-stop at consumer demonstrations and tastings around the world.

NUTRITIOUS & DELICIOUS™

www.nutritious-delicious.ca

ActiFry and you

And all of this is only the beginning. ActiFry is counting on you to continue to let us know your recipes. Your culinary talent can accompany ActiFry on its journeys, so do not hesitate to visit the Nutritious & Delicious site to add your recipes.

What

GERMANY

Doctor Johannes M. Peil, director of the Bad Nauheim Sports Clinic and chairman of the Sports Diet Institute

Vitamins, calories and fatty acids are all important factors considered when evaluating the nutritional value of foods. Yet, they do not necessarily correspond to pleasure and the criteria we use to make food choices on a daily basis. Taste, speed and ease of preparation are essential when we choose products that end up on our tables. With ActiFry family, you can combine speed, health, flavour and practicality. ActiFry family turns every kitchen into a gourmet health factory for the entire family. With ActiFry family, it is easier to follow recommendations from physicians and nutritionists to eat foods that are richer in nutrients, with more vitamins and minerals per calorie. And the pleasure is there. You do not have to give up your favourite foods. You get pleasure with health, and taste on the side.

RUSSIA

Doctor Mariana Trifonova, nutritionist

In Russia today, healthy eating corresponds to quality cooking that preserves food flavours and reduces cooking time. The Nutritious & Delicious product line is an absolute reference in the area. As a specialised user, I can confirm that it meets not only the standards set by dieticians, but also those standards Russians are looking for in household appliances, making it possible to cook delicious, high quality food. This combination responds precisely to the main principles of dietetic doctrine, which concerns not only the science of nutrition, but also the lifestyle to adopt.

professional say

CANADA

Kim Arrey, dietitian, nutritionist

Canadians today are always looking for new ways to eat healthy. The Nutritious and Delicious line from T-Fal allows you to eat healthy without sacrificing flavour, and at the same time reducing cooking time. As a dietitian (and working mom), I can confirm that the ActiFry family certainly fits the bill. The innovative Nutritious and Delicious products meet the standards set by dietitians and the demands set by busy health conscious Canadians. You can prepare some of your old favourites in a more healthy way without compromising the flavours that we all enjoy, or add some new easy way to prepare tasty meals to your repertoire.

FRANCE

Doctor Christian Recchia, physician, nutritionist

Eating is, above all, a social act of sharing, a moment of pleasure we constantly renew, but it is also an important moment of well being and health. Eating well is a good way to grow up better and to age better. ActiFry family's features make it possible to eat chips and potatoes with small quantities of fat, which helps fight obesity and cardiovascular diseases. ActiFry family also offers the possibility of cooking other foods well, such as vegetables, meat, fish, and fruit. This cookbook is an exciting concentration of flavourful, varied dishes cooked in a revolutionary appliance. The combinations were judiciously chosen to give you a maximum of satisfaction both taste-wise and nutrition-wise. All the recipes were carefully developed to take into account the nutritional properties of each ingredient, and their inclusion in a balanced menu.

Eating well with

Recommended Number of Food Guide Servings per Day

	Children			Teens		Adults			
Age in Years	2-3	4-8	9-13	14-18		19-50		51+	
Sex	Girls and Boys			Females	Males	Females	Males	Females	Males
Vegetables and fruit	4	5	6	7	8	7-8	8-10	7	7
Grain Product	3	4	6	6	7	6-7	8	6	7
Milk and Alternatives	2	2	3-2	3-4	3-4	2	2	3	3
Meat and Alternatives	1	1	1-2	2	3	2	3	2	3

The chart above shows how many Food Guide Servings you need from each of the four food groups every day. **Having the amount and type of food recommended and following the tips in Canada's Food Guide will help:**

- Meet your needs for vitamins, minerals and other nutrients.
- Reduce your risk of obesity, type 2 diabetes, heart disease, certain types of cancer and osteoporosis.
- Contribute to your overall health and vitality.

Canada's Food Guide

What is One Food Guide Serving?
Look at the examples below.

Fresh, frozen or canned vegetables	Leafy vegetables	Fresh, frozen or canned fruits	100% Juice
125 mL (1/2 cup)	Cooked: 125 mL (1/2 cup) Raw: 250 mL (1 cup)	1 fruit or 125 mL (1/2 cup)	125 mL (1/2 cup)

Bread	Bagel	Flat breads	Cooked rice, bulgur or quinoa	Cereal	Cooked pasta or couscous
1 slice (35 g)	1/2 bagel (45 g)	1/2 pita or 1/2 tortilla (35 g)	125 mL (1/2 cup)	Cold: 30 g Hot: 175 mL (3/4 cup)	125 mL (1/2 cup)

Milk or powdered milk (reconstituted)	Canned milk (evaporated)	Fortified soy beverage	Yogurt	Kefir	Cheese
250 mL (1 cup)	125 mL (1/2 cup)	250 mL (1 cup)	175 g (3/4 cup)	175 g (3/4 cup)	50 g (1 1/2 oz)

Cooked fish, shellfish, poultry, lean meat	Cooked legumes	Tofu	Eggs	Peanut or nut butters	Shelled nuts and seeds
75 g (2 1/2 oz)/125 mL (1/2 cup)	175 mL (3/4 cup)	150 g ou 175 mL (3/4 cup)	2 eggs	30 mL (2 Tbsp)	60 mL (1/4 cup)

Oils and fats

- Include a small amount – 30 to 45 mL (2 to 3 Tbsp) – of unsaturated fat each day. This includes oil used for cooking, salad dressings, margarine and mayonnaise.
- Use vegetable oils such as canola, olive and soybean.
- Choose soft margarines that are low in saturated and trans fats.
- Limit butter, hard margarine, lard ans shortening.

True or

Test what you know about the health benefits of the main nutrients found in your diet.

Protein just gives us energy.

False! *Protein is primarily essential for renewing body tissues and cells.*

Our cells need fat to function properly.

True! *Do not even think about avoiding fat entirely. Every day, we should eat 2 to 3 spoonfuls of a variety of fats, preferable from plants, to make sure we get the nutrients we need.*

Carbohydrates are sugars that we should avoid totally to stay trim.

False! *Bread, pasta, rice and grains provide slowly assimilated carbohydrates that give you the lasting energy you need, but also help you feel satiated so that you do not crave snacks between meals.*

Fibre is fattening!

False! *On the contrary, fibre from cauliflower, cucumbers, spinach, berries and grains helps digestion, reduces the amount of cholesterol you absorb, and regulates the speed at which you assimilate carbohydrates.*

Too little calcium is dangerous at any age.

True! *Throughout your life, you should eat cheese, yoghurt, fresh cheese, and cottage cheese to make sure you get enough calcium every day to maintain strong bones, help the muscles contract and prevent osteoporosis.*

There is iron not only in meat and offal, but also in oysters, eggs, pulses and dried fruit and nuts.

True! *It is essential to get the right amount of iron to produce red blood cells. However, keep in mind that you absorb iron from animal sources better.*

False?

You only find vitamin A in butter, cream and egg yolks.

You also find it in carrots, spinach, watercress, apricots and mangos as beta-carotene. It is an antioxidant that promotes growth, helps the eyes, skin and healing.

Vitamin C holds up well to cooking at high temperatures.

It is fragile, and requires slow, gentle steam cooking. You can find in it vegetables and fruit. It is an antioxidant that helps renew cells, promotes absorption of iron, and strengthens the immune system.

Without vitamin D, calcium cannot strengthen the bones.

True!

The body makes most of the vitamin D you need when you are exposed to the sun. The rest can be found in fish liver, oily fish, offal, egg yolks, whole milk and cheese.

Vitamin E is one of the anti-ageing antioxidants.

True!

You can find it in oil, dried fruit, nuts and seed, and it protects cell membranes and improves blood circulation.

B vitamins have many functions and are omnipresent.

True!

You find them in green vegetables, pulses, carrots, fish, meat, egg yolk and whole grains. They have an effect on the skin and hair, but also on the nervous system and the muscles, tissues and organs, and they contribute to making red blood cells.

Vary your diet as much as possible so that you get a wide variety of nutrients.

Why you should vary the oils you use

By using a variety of oils, you get a variety of flavours at the same time you get a variety of nutrients. That way, you can enjoy your food and eat healthfully at the same time. So why deprive yourself?

Food fats are made up of three kinds of fatty acids: *saturated* (SFA), which increase your bad cholesterol, unlike *monounsaturated* (MUFA) and *polyunsaturated* (PUFA), which contribute to a healthy cardiovascular system.

Generally speaking, limit your intake of saturated fatty acids: if you eat too much, they increase your bad cholesterol, or LDL, levels, which then clogs your arteries.

You find them in fat that hardens at room temperature, a sign that there is a large quantity of saturated fatty acids. They are in animal fat (butter, cream) and some vegetable oils (coconut, palm, shea butter).

It is better to choose vegetable oils, which are rich in monounsaturated and polyunsaturated fatty acids. These have different compositions.

As a result, it is ideal to use a variety of different oils to vary your nutrient intake (cf. the table) and benefits: olive, sunflower, rapeseed, walnut, hazelnut, and grape seed oil are examples of this vast and flavourful choice!

Monounsaturated Fat

Monounsaturated oils are called oleic oils because they contain more than 50% oleic acid. These include olive, sunflower, hazelnut, rapeseed, almond, pistachio, pecan, etc. Monounsaturated fatty acids form the myelin sheath around nerves, regulate the metabolism of fat and reduce LDL cholesterol levels. Our body can produce them from glucose.

Polyunsaturated Fat

These oils contain two types of *polyunsaturated fatty acids*: linoleic acid, a precursor of omega-6, and alpha-linoleic acid, a precursor of omega-3. These are long-chain fatty acids, whose protective properties are now recognized, and which the body cannot make by itself. It is essential to include them in your daily diet. That is why they are called *essential* fatty acids.

The benefits of

Omega 6

Linoleic acid helps lower your overall cholesterol level, lowering LDL and HDL cholesterol. It is essential for the formation of the skin's impermeable barrier and is part of several hormones. You find it in sunflower, corn and grape seed oils.

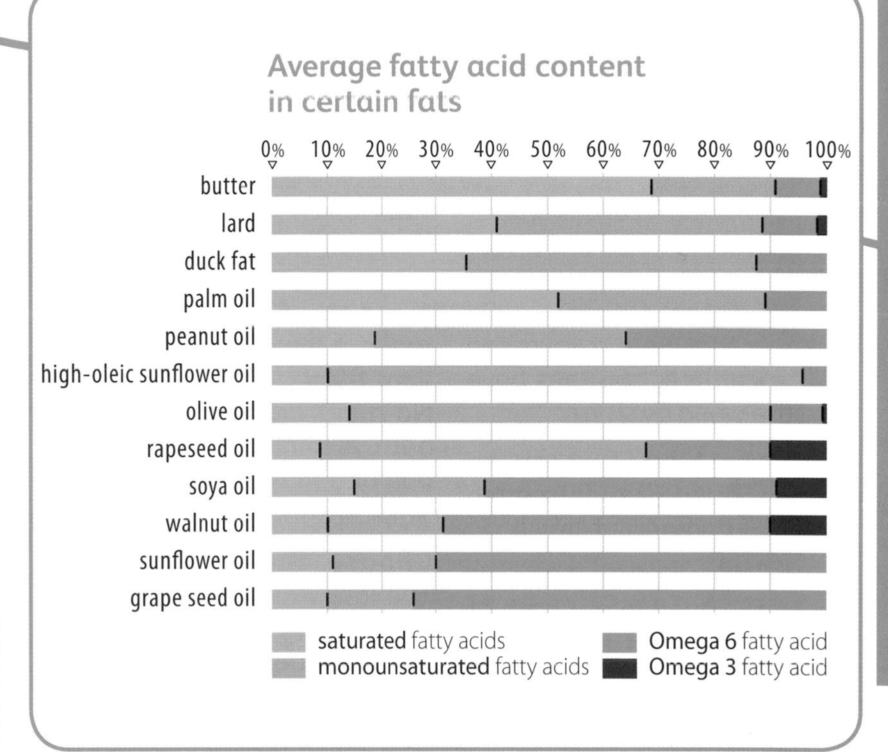

The benefits of

Omega 3

Alpha-linoleic acid reduces triglyceride levels in the blood and enables the synthesis of products that help the blood flow, protecting against cardiovascular disease. You find it in linseed, soya, walnut and lupin oils. Note: Rapeseed oil is both an oleic and a linoleic oil.

Choose the right fat!

Control both the quantity and quality.

Limit your overall fat and cholesterol intake by using little animal fat and a variety of vegetable oils.

Decrease saturated fatty acid intake.

Make sure you balance various fatty acids by choosing oils that contain unsaturated fatty acid, and especially polyunsaturated fatty acids.

Vary oils for more varied and complete intake of omega-3 and omega-6.

A short history of fries and potatoes

It is the potato that makes the fries! Everyone will eat fries, a crispy, festive treat people around the world love.

When, in the eighteenth century, an explorer named Parmentier brought the potato back with him from his distant travels, he did not know that he just invented fries! Since then, potatoes have taken the world by storm.

Potatoes are tubers that contain 80% water and 20% dry matter, composed primarily of starch.

What you need to know is that a fry dipped into a bath of hot oil loses part of the water it contains, which is replaced by fat. This explains the bad reputation fries have.

The ActiFry family solution. Thanks to its brilliant mixing and heating system, **1 spoon of oil is enough to make 3 lbs (1.5 kg) of crispy, light fries!**
No more odours, no more oil bath. A minimum of fat in the pan and in the fries. And a few simple instructions to follow.

Choose the right potato. The less water it contains and the more dry matter, the crispier the fry will be.

Yukon Gold, Russets and other high starch baking potatoes are ideal choices for homemade fries. Yukon Gold potatoes have the texture needed to make thicker, wedges-shaped fries. New potatoes often contain little sugar. However, as they are stored, their starch transforms into sugar. Fries then have a sweeter taste and are a darker brown (Agata, Monalisa).

Size: In Europe, people prefer small and medium-sized potatoes. Elsewhere, people prefer large potatoes.

Store potatoes in a cool (6° to 8°C), dark place.

There are more than 400 varieties of potatoes in Europe, and more than 4,000 in South America, where they have been cultivated in the Andes for more than 8,000 years.

In France, Belgium and Holland, you can find the "special fry" potato variety known as Bintje.

There are also other smaller, firm potatoes that work well: charlotte,

Potatoes are typically high on the Glycemic Index (GI), a scale ued to determine how foods raise blood sugar levels. Sweet potatoes are lower GI for those looking to control blood sugar levels and can be a nutritious and delicious option to prepare Actifry.

Potatoes with low amounts of dry matter (waxy potatoes) make soft fries; these include Agata, spunta.

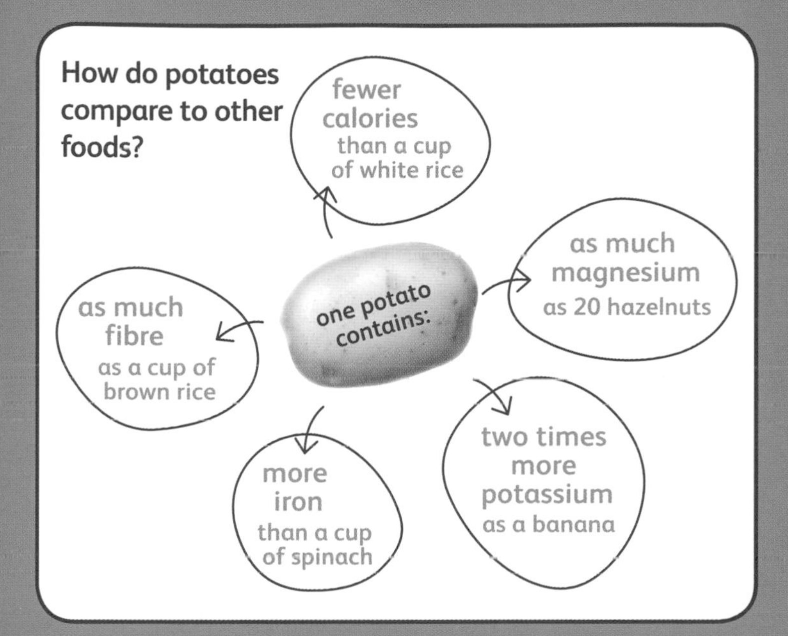

Making fries with ActiFry

Choose special fry potato varieties.

If you are using baby new potatoes, add a few extra minutes to the recommended cooking time.

If you are using frozen fries, which are generally precooked, there is no need to add oil.

How to prepare potatoes for fries in the ActiFry

The potatoes should not stick to each other. How do you avoid this? After peeling the potatoes, wash them under running water before cutting them into fries. Wash them again after cutting to remove as much starch as possible. Dry the fries thoroughly using a very absorbent, dry tea towel. Make sure your fries are very dry before putting them in the ActiFry.

How to store potatoes to make fries in the ActiFry

The best place to keep potatoes is in a cellar or another cool (between 6° and 8°C), dark place.

How to cut potatoes for fries in the ActIFry

Very important! Your fries will be more or less crisp or moist depending on how you cut them. The thinner you cut them, the crispier they will be. The thicker you cut them, the moister they will be inside. Vary the cut according to your taste:

- thin: 8 x 8 mm
- standard: 10 x 10 mm
- thick: 13 x 13 mm

Do not add too much salt! Try using spices or herbs instead of salt.

Potatoes: They are all good!

As long as fries are made will only a little bit of fat, there is not reason not to eat them. On the contrary, they are a little treat that makes it easier to negotiate with yourself and your children to eat less fat and sugar in the rest of your diet without feeling punished or on a diet.

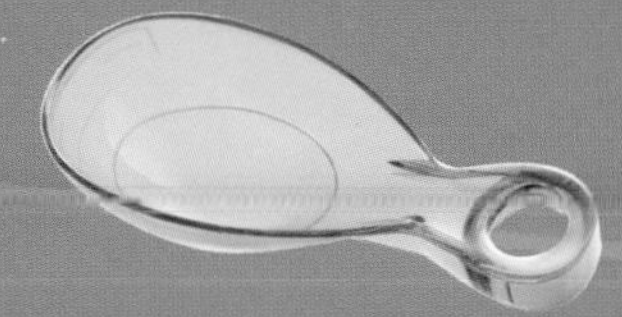

Balance

Balanced menus for the week

You do not build a balanced diet based on a single meal, but over a whole week!

It is essential to vary your menus

That is why this recipe book provides you with a number of original recipes spread out over two weeks of balanced meals. They are simple to make and, with ActiFry, they respect the flavour and nutritional properties of the food.

Breakfast is a key moment in the day and important to your nutritional balance

By building a good first meal of the day, you not only replenish after a long night of fasting, but you also ensure that you will have an effective morning without snacking and cravings.

We suggest an ideally balanced breakfast based on **four essential pillars: a beverage, a dairy product, a grain product and fruit,** eaten whole, as juice or stewed.

Whatever your preference, make sure that each of these four groups is included on your morning breakfast. It is important to select products carefully for their nutritional value and flavours, so that this useful breakfast is the first delicious moment in your day!

Lunch and dinner should each provide ⅓ of your daily needs.

These include a starter, main dish (fish or meat with starch and green vegetables), cheese/dairy product and a piece of fruit. The secret to varying your diet is knowing that moderation is key.

is Key

Nathalie HUTTER LARDEAU
Nutritionist

I have good news! You no longer have to choose between a balanced diet and enjoying what you eat. This is important when you have to come up with meals that will satisfy the whole family. ActiFry family adapts its capacity to a family's needs and portion sizes. Its main strong point is being able to cook not only fries but also a number of delicious, easy-to-make dishes using a minimum of fat. It is a really useful tool!

As a nutritionist, I see parents struggling daily to eat less fat and less sugar, to watch their children's and their own weight. I see people succeed for a period of time, more or less long, and then give up. They break down and return to old habits that are bad for their own health and their family's in the short or long term.

ActiFry family makes it possible to modify how you eat without radical changes. It makes it possible to cook with less fat and not even notice.

In ActiFry family, you can make 3 lbs (1.5 kg) of crispy, golden fries with a single spoonful of oil.

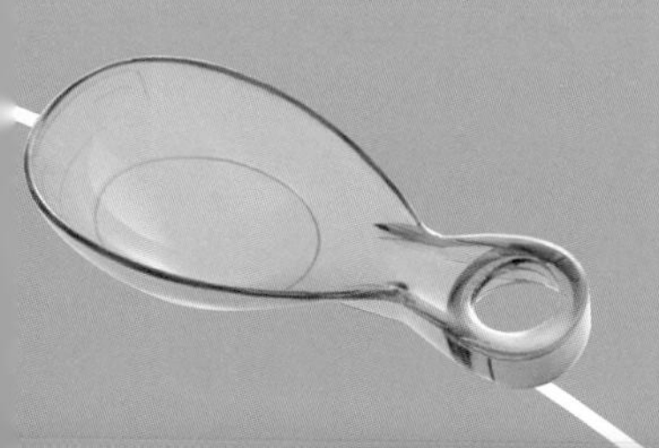

All you need to do to naturally, effortlessly balance your diet is to vary your enjoyment and the food you eat using the menus we have carefully designed for the whole family: meat, fish, vegetables and fruit can be found in all our recipes.

You will find savoury and sweet recipes, all with a minimum of fat, easy to make, and that can cook all by themselves in the ActiFry. There are recipes that will introduce children to new flavours. There are exotic and original recipes to please difficult teenagers.

There are enough recipes to rebalance the entire family's diet, smoothly and easily. You can do it and still eat chips! You will not even have to talk about the transition, it will come so naturally.

Balance should be lasting if you want to prevent excess weight and related health problems.

When you cook low-fat food every day in your ActiFry family, you are cooking for the future. It is vital for your health and for that of your family.

Week 1:

The recipes listed in green are detailed in this book.

	Monday *Jump-start day!*	Tuesday *Your choice*	Wednesday *Lunch with the kids*
Breakfast	Hot chocolate Bread, butter and honey Kiwi	Green jasmine tea Mixed grain Melba toast and jam Flavoured yoghurt Orange juice	Coffee Bowl of cereal with milk Stewed fruit
Lunch	Coleslaw salad ActiFried Kebab (p. 111) Mashed potatoes with carrots Low-fat cottage cheese Fruit salad	Cucumbers and cream Swordfish and Basil Croquettes (p. 48) Rice and broccoli Camembert cheese Sliced pineapple	Baby green salad with tomatoes and walnuts Chicken drumsticks Real Homemade Fries (p. 28) Cottage cheese + banana cubes
Dinner	Italian-style Vegetables (p. 132) Fresh pasta Cooked ham Fruit yoghurt	Stir-fried vegetables with mushrooms and bacon Semolina Halva (p. 55)	ActiFried Scrambled Tortilla (p. 83) Raw vegetable plate (green salad, grated carrots, beets) Emmental cheese Seasonal fruit

balanced meals

Thursday *On the run!*	Friday *Evening with friends*	Saturday *Your choice*	Sunday *Family meal*
Chicory Bread, butter Cottage cheese and dried fruit and nuts	Capuccino Bowl of cereal with milk Cream cheese ½ grapefruit	Caramel tea French bread with cheese Mixed berry salad de fruits rouges	Viennese coffee Croissant Vanilla yogurt Homemade smoothie
Tabouleh Very Spicy Creole Prawns (p. 79) Zucchinis and eggplant gratin Seasonal fruit	Red cabbage salad with wholegrain mustard Spicy Chicken Drumsticks (p. 72) Cumin quinoa Plain yoghurt Poached pear	Tomato, feta and basil salad Chicken Shawarma (p. 43) Stir-fried vegetables with brown rice Peaches in syrup	Marinière Mussels with Cherry Tomatoes and Basil (p. 120) Mixed green salad with balsamic vinegar vinaigrette Grape clafoutis (with green and red grapes)
 Red Beans with Tomato Sauce (p. 51) Minced beef Berry salad and custard sauce	1 slice smoked salmon on mixed grain bread with lemon zest Green Beans with Fresh Sage and Almonds (p. 131) Cream cheese Mango wedges	Grated Vegetable Terrine with Lemon and Chives (p. 135) Soft-boiled eggs with bread soldiers Yogurt with hazelnuts and apricots	Steamed shrimp dumplings FriedRice (p. 84) Cream cheese with litchis

Week 2:

The recipes listed in green are detailed in this book.

	Monday *Rebalancing day*	Tuesday *Your choice*	Wednesday *Dinner with friends*
Breakfast	Coffee with milk Wholemeal bread, butter and honey Stewed fruit	Peppermint and lemon balm tea Bowl of cereal, milk and banana cubes	Coffee Mixed grain Melba toast, jam Cream cheese Orange or grapefruit juice
Lunch	Grated carrots with lemon Salmon steak with whole grain mustard Split pea purée Skim milk mozzarella Apricots with Almonds (p. 140)	Avocado Spicy Rabbit (p. 104) Polenta and cherry tomatoes Plain yoghurt Seasonal fruit	Radishes Veal escalope with light cream sauce Pumpkin and nutmeg purée Wholemeal bread ActiFried Apples and Bananas with Lime and Coriander (p. 144)
Dinner	Spanish-style ActiFried Tofu (p. 128) Rocket salad Blue cheese Fruit salad	Prawns and grapefruit Mediterranean Vegetable Stir-fry (p. 123) Apple tart Glass of milk	Shirred eggs with smoked salmon Potatoes with Mushrooms (p. 35) Cottage cheese Stewed apples with rhubarb

balanced meals

Thursday *Your choice*	Friday *Energy breakfast!*	Saturday *Party night*	Sunday *Pleasure and cuisine day*
Capucchino French bread + honey Glass of milk Kiwi	Vanilla tea Bowl of cereal with milk Stewed fruit	Cinnamon tea Brioche Fromage frais and fruit sauce	Hot chocolate Crêpes with jam Fruit salad
Green cabbage and apple salad ✧ **Pork Sticks (p. 67)** Seasonal vegetable strips Swiss cheese Vanilla custard	Grated beetroot ✧ **Beef Stroganoff (p. 64)** Chili sauce Flavoured fromage frais	Raw vegetable plate ✧ **Lamb Tajine Preserved Lemons and Black Olives (p. 96)** Brown semolina Fromage blanc or cottage cheese Seasonal fruit	Green salad ✧ **Fried Fish with Tartar Sauce (p. 47)** Stir-fried courgettes Panna cotta with berries
✧ **Sun-dried Tomato and Scallion Risotto (p. 124)** Citrus compote	 ✧ **Bolognaise Sauce (p. 100)** Fresh pasta Grated cheese Seasonal fruit	Croque-monsieur cheese melt Seasonal vegetable strips ✧ **Cinnamon Apples (p. 56)**	Tzatziki, tarama and multi-grain toast Cherry tomatoes, carrot sticks and fresh cheese sauce Tomato juice ✧ **Lavander Nectarines (p. 139)**

Kids in the Kitchen

Moments of discovery

Nutritional information per serving
[Protein: 5.2 g Fat: 2.5 g Carbohydrates: 41.5 g]
[Sodium: 0.02 g]

Nutritious

Potatoes are starches that provide you with complex carbohydrates and keep you from feeling hungry between meals. Complex carbohydrates should be part of every meal. With ActiFry, you can cook them with very little fat and using good quality oil.

Real Homemade Fries

Serves **6** • Preparation **15** min • Cooking **45** min

1 Ask mum to cut the potatoes into strips the size you like most: ⅓ x ⅓ inch, ½ x ½ inch or ⅔ x ⅔ inch. Wash the cut Fries well, drain and dry carefully with a clean tea towel.

2 Put the Fries into the ActiFry pan. Mum will pour the oil over the fries. They will be cooked in 45 minutes. Add salt. They are ready.

Cooking times can vary depending on the kind of potato you use and how thick the fries are cut.

198 Cal

Did you know?
Potatoes rank fourth on the list of the most-grown foods
in the world, coming in after rice, wheat and corn.

Did you know?
Almonds are fruits of almond trees.
Once they are dried, they are used in many different ways,
including whole, toasted, flaked,
ground, as a paste, as a cream,
as milk and as a sweet beverage.
Ground almonds

Nutritional information per serving
[Protein: 6.7 g Fat: 10.2 g Carbohydrates: 42.8 g]
[Sodium: 0.02 g]

Nutritious

Yes, this recipe contains starches. But it also has a good quantity of essential fatty acids, from the hazelnut oil and the almonds, which contribute to a healthy nervous system.

Almond Fries

Serves **6** • Preparation **15** min • Cooking **45** min

- **3 lb** (**1.5 kg**) potatoes, peeled and washed
- 1 vegetable oil
- 2 hazelnut oil
- 3 ground almonds

1. Ask mum to cut the potatoes into fries ½ inch thick. Wash the cut French Fries well, drain and dry carefully with a clean tea towel.
2. Mix the oils in a bowl with the ground almonds.
3. Put the fries in the ActiFry pan, and mum will pour the almond and oil mixture evenly over them. They'll be ready in 45 minutes!

Nutritional information per serving
[Protein: 9.3 g Fat: 21.7 g Carbohydrates: 53.8 g]
[Sodium: 0.9 g]

Nutritious

Vary this recipe by adding other ingredients, such as peanuts and bacon-flavoured snack puffs, to your potatoes. Your family will get their fill of complex carbohydrates, but this recipe is also a treat. Save it for special occasions.

Peanut Bacon Fries

Serves **6** • Preparation **20** min • Cooking **55** min

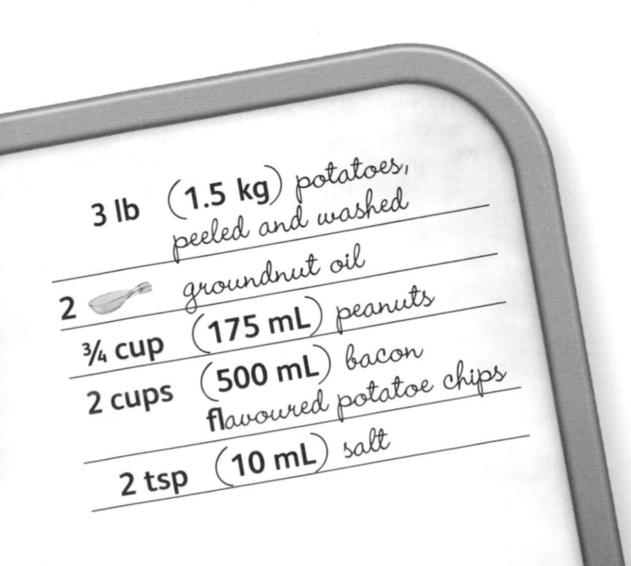

1. Ask mum to cut the potatoes into fries ½ inch thick. Wash the cut fries well, drain and dry carefully with a clean tea towel. Put the fries in the ActiFry pan, and mum will add the oil. Cook for 45 minutes.
2. Ask mum to use a food processor to grind the fries into a powder with the salt. Meanwhile, chop the peanuts. Mix everything together.
3. After 45 minutes, mum will open the ActiFry and spread this mixture over the fries. Cook for another 10 minutes and then they are ready.

430 cal
Did you know?
The groundnut or peanut plant is an annual that buries its fruits after they have been fertilized; these fruits are called groundnuts or peanuts. The plant originated in Mexico.
Peanuts and chips

225 Cal
Did you know?
There are 50,000 species of mushrooms,
but only a few hundred of them are edible.

Nutritional information per serving
[Protein: 5.9 g Fat: 9.2 g Carbohydrates: 32.8 g]
[Sodium: 0.03 g]

Nutritious

The potatoes in this recipe contribute complex carbohydrates to your diet. These are your body's main source of fuel and keep you from craving snacks between meals.

Potatoes with Mushrooms

Serves **6** • Preparation **5** min • Cooking **47** min

2 lb (1 kg) potatoes, peeled and washed
8 oz (250 g) button mushrooms, cut into quarters
1 onion, finely chopped
¾ cup (175 mL) 18% table cream
1 vegetable oil
Salt and pepper

1. Ask mum to cut the potatoes into cubes. Wash the cut cubes well, drain and dry carefully with a clean tea towel.
2. Mum will heat the oil in the ActiFry and then add the onions and cook them for 7 minutes. When they start to look transparent, add the potato cubes. Cook for 25 to 30 minutes, until the potatoes are nearly cooked.
3. Add the mushrooms and cook another 7 minutes. Pour in the cream and cook for 2 to 3 minutes. Mum will season with salt and pepper.

Nutritional information per serving
[Protein: 4.8 g Fat: 12.9 g Carbohydrates: 36.7 g]
[Sodium: 0.02 g]

Nutritious

Despite popular belief, goose and duck fat are fairly well balanced in terms of fatty acids. This means that occasionally you can use them for cooking, because they add a nice flavour the whole family will appreciate. With ActiFry, you can cook potatoes using very little fat.

Sarladaise Potatoes

Serves **6** • Preparation **20** min • Cooking **47** min

- **2 ½ lb (1.25 kg)** potatoes, peeled and washed
- **5** [spoon] duck or goose fat
- **5** cloves garlic, finely chopped
- **1** bunch parsley, finely chopped
- Salt and pepper

1. Ask mum to cut the potatoes into ⅛ inch (3 mm) thick slices. Wash the potato slices well, drain and dry with a clean tea towel.
2. Mum will melt the fat in the ActiFry for 2 minutes, then you can add the potato slices. Cook for 35 minutes.
3. Add the garlic to the pan and cook for 10 minutes. Sprinkle with parsley and season.

— 272 Cal
Did you know?
Garlic is a rather large herbaceous plant (which means it is herb-shaped).
We eat the root,
which forms cloves that are
used as a condiment.

Nutritious

This recipe combines the benefits of new potatoes (vitamins, minerals and complex carbohydrates), prawns (good quality protein and little fat) and the beneficial effects of garlic to help blood circulation. New potatoes have more vitamin C than other potatoes, along with more minerals such as magnesium, which fights stress. You preserve these properties better when you do not peel the potatoes. The potatoes in this recipe help your children appreciate prawns.

Did you know?

Tomatoes are not vegetables, but fruits. They come in many varieties and shapes: round or long, red and yellow, plum tomatoes, cherry tomatoes, vine tomatoes and even beef tomatoes.

Nutritional information per serving
[Protein: 11.5 g Fat: 7.8 g Carbohydrates: 45.2 g]
[Sodium: 0.4 g]

New Potatoes with Garlic, Sun-dried Tomatoes and Prawns

Serves **6** • Preparation **25** min • Cooking **45** min

- **2 lb** (**1 kg**) new potatoes
- **20** cloves garlic, unpeeled
- **3** [spoon] olive oil
- **20** sun-dried tomatoes in oil
- **20** uncooked prawns, peeled
- **½ cup** (**125 mL**) bunch parsley, finely chopped
- **2** large pinches fine sea salt

1 Wash the potatoes without peeling them and dry them well.

2 Ask mum to pour the oil into the ActiFry. Add the whole new potatoes and the garlic. Cook for 35 minutes.

3 Add the prawns, sun-dried tomatoes and salt, and cook for 10 minutes. Add the parsley right before serving.

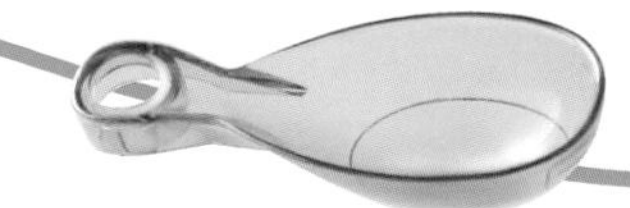

Wiener Schnitzel

Serves **6** • Preparation **20** min • Cooking **15** min

This recipe is a perfect marriage of good quality protein (veal) for strong muscles, balanced fatty acids (rapeseed oil and veal) to keep the cardiovascular system running smoothly, and complex carbohydrates (flour, breadcrumbs) so you feel full. Ideally, you should serve this dish with spinach or a salad.

- **1 ½ lb** (**750 g**) veal escalopes, cut into small, **1 oz** pieces (**30 g**)
- **3x1** [spoon] grapeseed oil or canola oil (1 per batch)
- **1 ¼ cups** (**300 mL**) dried breadcrumbs
- **⅔ cup** (**150 mL**) all-purpose flour
- **6** eggs, beaten
- **2** lemons, juiced
- Salt and pepper

1 Coat the veal escalopes first with flour, then dip in the beaten egg and finally coat with the breadcrumbs. Repeat these same steps a second time and ask mum to put the coated veal pieces in the refrigerator for 30 minutes.

2 Mum will heat a spoon of rapeseed oil in the ActiFry and add a batch of meat, placed flat in the pan, to cook for 10 to 15 minutes.

3 Continue cooking batches until all the meat is cooked.

Tip: Add a little water to the beaten egg yolks for the egg dip.

417 Cal

Did you know?

Dried breadcrumbs are nothing more than dried bread, that has been crushed. They are used to coat foods, to thicken sauces and to sprinkle on top of dished made au gratin.

166 Cal
Did you know?
The word vinegar comes from the Old French words meaning "sour wine".
Vinegar is made from wine that is left to age
and turn sour.
Marinade

Nutritional information per serving
[Protein: 23.6 g Fat: 4.9 g Carbohydrates: 7.6 g]
[Sodium: 1.5 g]

Nutritious

This recipe provides good quality proteins for healthy muscles, and is a great way for your children to discover new flavours.

Chicken shawarma

Serves **6** • Preparation **10** min • Cooking **10-15** min

- 1 ½ lb (750 g) boneless, skinned chicken breasts
- 1 [spoon] ground cumin
- 1 [spoon] Ras el hanout spice blend (or shawarma spices)
- 3 cloves garlic, finely chopped
- 2 onion, finely chopped
- 2 [spoon] vinegar
- 2 [spoon] vegetable oil
- Salt and pepper

1 Ask mum to slice the chicken.

2 Mix all the ingredients together and put in the refrigerator for 12 hours so they marinate well.

3 Add the marinated chicken to the ActiFry pan and cook for 10 to 15 minutes. Season to taste.

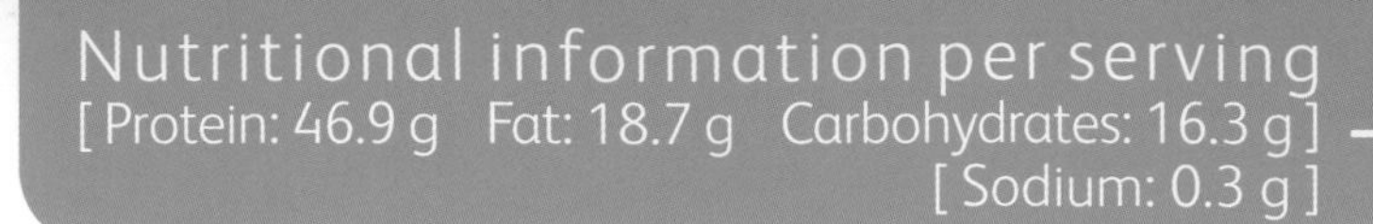
Nutritional information per serving
[Protein: 46.9 g Fat: 18.7 g Carbohydrates: 16.3 g]
[Sodium: 0.3 g]

Fried Meatballs

Serves **6** • Preparation **15** min • Cooking **20** min

Nutritious

ActiFry makes flavourful meatballs without adding any fat. Using cheese is a good way to contribute to the day's calcium intake. Calcium is particularly important for children to grow and have strong bones.

- **2 lb (1 kg)** minced meat (mixture of 60% veal and 40% pork)
- **2** [spoon] cumin
- **5 oz (150 g)** Gruyère cheese or other hard cheese
- **3** slices white bread
- **⅔ cup (150 mL)** skim milk
- **2** eggs
- **½ cup (125 mL)** bunch parsley, finely chopped
- **⅔ cup (150 mL)** plain flour
- **1** [spoon] grapeseed oil or canola oil
- Salt and pepper

1 Soak the bread in the skimmed milk. Ask mum to mix the minced meat in a bowl with the ground cumin, chopped parsley, eggs, the soaked bread, salt and pepper.

2 Help mum make meatballs that are 1.5 inch (4 cm) in diameter. Add a piece of gruyère cheese in the middle of each meatball. Make sure you seal the meatballs well so that the cheese does not drip out during cooking.

3 Roll the meatballs in the flour and cook them with the oil for 20 minutes in the ActiFry.

431 Cal

Did you know?
Bread is made from flour, water, salt and yeast.
The crust in the harder, darker outside surrounding a soft inside.
Cheese
Flour

426 Cal
Nutritious
Fish is very nutritious, because it contains protein, fatty acids and iodine. This recipe will help your children learn to like it.
Did you know?
There are three different kinds of pepper:
Green pepper, or pepper plant fruits that are harvested before they are ripe.
White pepper, or ripe pepper plant fruits with the skin removed.
Black pepper, or ripe pepper plant fruits with the skin, fermented and then dried.
Flour
Tartar sauce

Nutritional information per serving
[Protein: 33.5 g Fat: 22.3 g Carbohydrates: 21.3 g]
[Sodium: 0.3 g]

Fried Whitebait with Tartar Sauce

Fry:

- **2 lb (1 kg)** whitebait
- **1 cup (250 mL)** all-purpose flour
- **4** [measuring spoon] good quality oil
- Salt, pepper

Tartar sauce:

- **1 cup (250 mL)** sour cream
- **6** gherkins, finely chopped
- **4** [measuring spoon] capers, finely chopped
- **2** lemons, juiced
- **2** shallots, finely chopped
- **2** [measuring spoon] flat-leaf parsley, finely chopped
- Salt and pepper

Serves **6** • Preparation **15** min
• Cooking **10-15** min
depending on the size of the fish

1 Prepare the tartar sauce by mixing all the ingredients together and seasoning to taste.

2 Ask mum to wash and pat dry the little whole fish. Coat with flour and season. Put the fish in the ActiFry pan, pour in the oil and cook for 10 to 15 minutes or until they are golden and crispy.

3 Mum will remove them the pan and drain them on paper towels. Serve with the tartar sauce.

Nutritional information per serving
[Protein: 26.9 g Fat: 13.8 g Carbohydrates: 24.8 g]

[Sodium: 0.2 g]

Nutritious

This tasty dish combines fish protein and egg protein. This mixture of flavours will please young and old alike.

Swordfish and Basil Croquettes

Serves **6** • Preparation **15** min • Cooking **12** min

- 1 ¼ lb (625 g) swordfish, cooked and flaked
- 3 slices white bread
- ⅔ cup (150 mL) 18% table cream
- 2 eggs
- 1 large bunch basil, finely chopped
- 1 cup (250 mL) plain flour
- 1 olive oil
- Salt and pepper

1. Ask mum to mix the swordfish with half the oil, the bread that was first soaked in the cream, the eggs and the seasoning.
2. Add the basil and shape into croquettes, each about 1.5 inch large (4 cm) each, using a plastic pastry bag.
3. Coat each croquette with flour and mum can put them into the ActiFry to cook in hot oil for about 12 minutes.

Tip: Make small, compact croquettes and do not cook too many at a time.

— 339 Cal

Did you know?
Cream is milk fat.
Originally, crème fraîche was a French speciality.
Flour

176 Cal
Did you know?
Beans are the fruit of a Central and South American plant.
The word "bean" refers to the fruit, the seed and the plant.

Nutritional information per serving
[Protein: 7.7 g Fat: 4.5 g Carbohydrates: 27.7 g]
[Sodium: 0.4 g]

Nutritious

Grains such as red beans are a very interesting source of plant protein which, although less complete in terms of amino acids than plant protein, is an essential part of our diet. This dish makes an ideal dinner for kids.

Red Beans with Tomato Sauce

Serves **6** • Preparation **15** min • Cooking **25** min

3 cups (750 mL) canned red beans
2 onions, chopped
½ cup (125 mL) strained tomato purée
2 cloves garlic, finely chopped
⅔ cup (150 mL) vegetable broth
2 vegetable oil
Salt and pepper

1. Ask mum to heat the oil and cook the cook the onions and garlic for 5 minutes.
2. Drain the red beans and add them to the ActiFry along with the tomato passata and the vegetable broth.
3. Mum can season the dish, then cook for 20 minutes.

Optional: If you add minced meat when you start the cooking, then you get chilli.

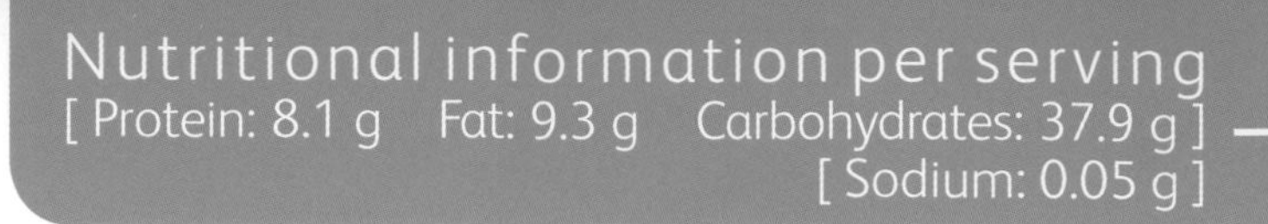

Nutritional information per serving
[Protein: 8.1 g Fat: 9.3 g Carbohydrates: 37.9 g]
[Sodium: 0.05 g]

Nutritious

Zucchinis have few calories and are full of vitamins, minerals and fibre. This recipe also contains calcium from the yogurt. Do not hesitate to serve with a starchy food.

Zucchinis with Yogurt Sauce

Serves **6** • Preparation **15** min • Cooking **9** min

2 lb (**1 kg**) zucchinis cut into ¾ inch (2 cm) cubes

1 ¾ cups (**425 mL**) all-purpose flour

4 [scoops] sunflower oil

Yogurt sauce:

¾ cup (**175 mL**) plain fat free yogurt

4 cloves garlic, finely chopped

2 [scoops] finely chopped dill

Salt and pepper

1 Roll the zucchini cubes in the flour to coat lightly. Tap to remove the excess flour.

2 Ask mum to heat the oil in the ActiFry for 2 minutes, and then add the cubes of seasoned zucchinis. Cook for 7 minutes.

3 Prepare the sauce by adding garlic and dill to the yogurt and mixing well. Mum will add salt and pepper.

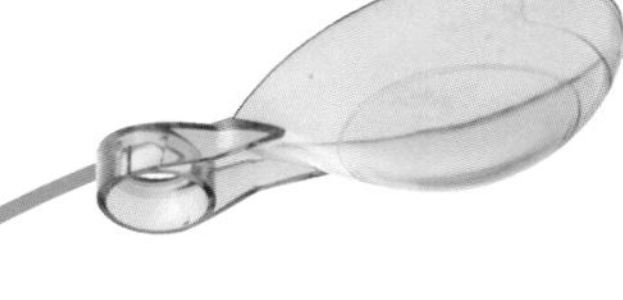

262 Cal

Did you know?
Zucchinis are a kind of squash that you harvest very young, before they are fully ripe.
The squash family includes pumpkins, custard marrow and winter squash.
Yogurt sauce

253 Cal
Did you know?
Semolina is a kind of grainy flour made from hard wheat.
It is used to make semolina cakes, soups and couscous.
It is also used to make pasta.

Nutritional information per serving
[Protein: 6.8 g Fat: 8.4 g Carbohydrates: 37.7 g]
[Sodium: 0.02 g]

Nutritious

This dessert is a useful treat, which allows you to complete your supplies of complex carbohydrates and calcium. In addition, almonds contain antioxidants and essential fatty acids.

Semolina Halva

Serves **6** • Preparation **15** min • Cooking **25** min

- 1 ⅔ cups (400 mL) semolina
- ⅓ cup (75 mL) blanched almonds
- 1 (spoon) olive oil
- 1 (spoon) butter
- 1 (spoon) water (to moisten the semolina)
- 3 (spoons) granulated sugar
- 1 cup (250 mL) skim milk + ½ cup (125 mL) hot water
- ½ (spoon) vanilla extract

1. Mix the semolina, olive oil, water and almonds. Ask mum to put the mixture in the ActiFry and cook for 15 min.
2. Mix the vanilla and sugar in hot water and add the milk. Pour this mixture over the semolina and almond mixture. Cook for 10 minutes.
3. After 10 minutes, ask mum to put the semolina in a bowl and cover with a tea towel for 10 minutes so the semolina can finish cooking.

Tip: Sprinkle with sugar right before serving.

Nutritional information per serving
[Protein: 0.8 g Fat: 4.4 g Carbohydrates: 33.6 g]
[Sodium: 0 g]

Nutritious

This dessert is a healthy, delicious way to end a meal and corresponds to two portions of fruit. The apples are particularly interesting for their pectin content: this fibre helps you feel full.

Cinnamon Apples

Serves **6** • Preparation **20** min • Cooking **25** min

- **6** Golden Delicious apples, washed and peeled
- **½ cup (125 mL)** dried apricots, chopped
- **1 tsp (5 mL)** ground cinnamon
- **2** granulated sugar
- **2** sunflower oil

1. Ask mum to cut the apples into wedges, to remove the skins and to put them in the ActiFry with the oil. Cook for 20 minutes.
2. Add the apricots and cook for 5 more minutes, or until the apples are tender.
3. Mix the sugar and cinnamon to serve with the hot apples.

— 162 Cal

Teen Years

A time of complicity and sharing…

Nutritional information per serving
[Protein: 5.2 g Fat: 6.8 g Carbohydrates: 41.5 g]
[Sodium: 0.02 g]

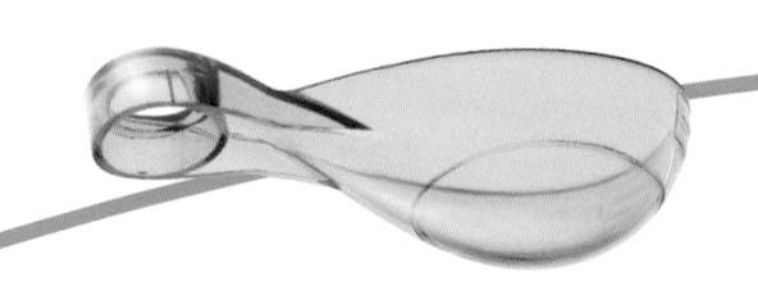

Nutritious

Chips with less fat but more taste. That is a good way to convince teens to adopt ActiFry.

Curry Fries

Serves **6** • Preparation **15** min • Cooking **45** min

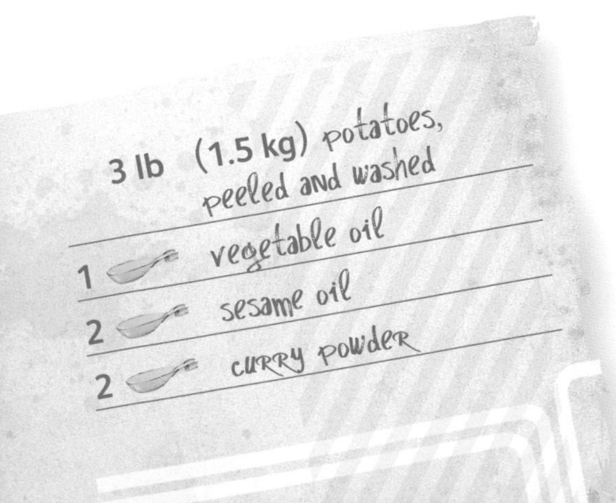

3 lb (1.5 kg) potatoes, peeled and washed
1 [spoon] vegetable oil
2 [spoon] sesame oil
2 [spoon] curry powder

1. Cut the potatoes into fries ½ inch (1 cm) thick. Wash the cut fries well, drain and dry carefully.
2. Mix the vegetable oil, sesame oil and curry powder.
3. Put the fries in the ActiFry pan and pour the oil and curry mixture evenly over them. Cook for 45 minutes.

236 Cal

199 Cal
OMÉGAS ESSENTIELS
Lesieur
isio 4

Nutritional information per serving
[Protein: 5.3 g Fat: 2.5 g Carbohydrates: 41.5 g]
[Sodium: 0.04 g]

Nutritious

Put an end to snacking! These fries will stop between-meal cravings and are so tasty, you can't resist them.

Tex-Mex Fries

Serves **6** • Preparation **15** min • Cooking **55** min

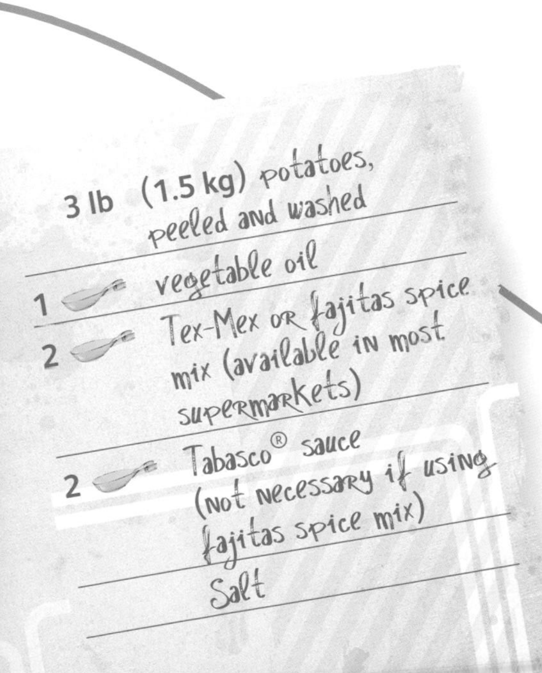

3 lb (1.5 kg) potatoes, peeled and washed

1 vegetable oil

2 Tex-Mex or fajitas spice mix (available in most supermarkets)

2 Tabasco® sauce (not necessary if using fajitas spice mix)

Salt

1. Cut the potatoes into ½ inch (1 cm) thick fries, wash well and dry carefully.
2. Mix the Tex-Mex powder with the vegetable oil in a small bowl. Put the fries in the ActiFry pan and pour the spice mixture evenly over them. Cook for 45 minutes.
3. Open the ActiFry, add salt and pour the Tabasco® over the fries. Cook for another 10 minutes.

Nutritional information per serving
[Protein: 35.9 g Fat: 19 g Carbohydrates: 7.1 g]
[Sodium: 0.1 g]

Nutritious

Beef is a good source of iron and vitamin B12, which fights anaemia.

Beef Stroganoff

Serves **6** • Preparation **10** min • Cooking **10** min

- 2 lb (1 kg) beef tenderloin
- 2 [spoon] vegetable oil
- 2 large onions sliced
- 2 [spoon] paprika
- ⅔ cup (150 mL) 18% table cream
- Salt and pepper

1. Cut the beef into thin slices and mix with the paprika.
2. Heat the oil in the ActiFry and then add the onions and cook for 4 minutes. Add the beef and cook for 3-4 minutes.
3. Add the cream, boil for 2 minutes, season and serve.

348 Cal

246 Cal

Nutritional information per serving
[Protein: 35.8 g Fat: 9.1 g Carbohydrates: 3.2 g]
[Sodium: 0.6 g]

Nutritious

Contrary to popular belief, pork is not that fatty if you choose the right cut, and it has balanced fatty acids.

Pork Sticks

Serves **6** • Preparation **15** min • Cooking **25** min

- 2 lb (1 kg) pork loin, cut into sticks
- 4 oyster sauce
- 3 soya sauce
- 1 sugar
- 1 cooking oil

1. Marinate the pork in a mixture of oyster sauce, soya sauce, oil and sugar for one hour.
2. Put the pork and the marinade in the ActiFry. Cook for 25 minutes.

Tip: Serve with fried rice.

Nutritional information per serving
[Protein: 30.4 Fat: 20.5 g Carbohydrates: 12.2 g]
[Sodium: 0.4 g]

Veal Croquettes with Cream

Serves **6** • Preparation **20** min • Cooking **12** min

Nutritious

Veal is a lean meat that contains good quality protein along with vitamin B12, which helps fight anaemia. These croquettes are ideal for the entire family: kids love the shape, and so do teens.

- 1 ¼ lb (625 g) veal, finely minced
- ⅔ cup (150 mL) 18% table cream
- 4 slices white bread
- 1 cup (250 mL) finely chopped parsley
- ¾ cup (175 mL) grated parmesan cheese
- 2 whole eggs
- 3x1 olive oil
- Salt and pepper

1 Soak the bread in a quarter of the cream and then mix it with the minced veal in a bowl.

2 Add the eggs, parmesan, parsley and seasoning. Make croquettes, each using 2 tsp (30 mL) of the mixture each.

3 Heat a spoonful of oil in the ActiFry pan and cook the croquettes in a single layer for 8 minutes. Add the remaining cream and continue cooking for 4 minutes. Season.

Tip: Do not cook too many at once. It is better to cook them in batches.

360 Cal

386 Cal

Nutritious

Turkey is a kind of poultry that has a large amount of quality protein, with the advantage of having little fat, and the fatty acids it contains are primarily monounsaturated and polyunsaturated, which contribute to a healthy cardiovascular system. Peppers contain a lot of vitamins, particularly vitamin C.

Nutritional information per serving
[Protein: 39.6 g Fat: 11.9 g Carbohydrates: 25.3 g]
[Sodium: 0.1 g]

Turkey Breast with Three Peppers

Serves **6** • Preparation **20** min • Cooking **35** min

- 2 lb (1 kg) turkey breast cut into 1 inch x ½ inch (2.5 x 1 cm)
- 6 peppers (2 red, 2 green, 2 yellow), seeded
- 2 onions, sliced
- 4 cloves garlic, finely chopped
- 3 [spoon] olive oil
- ½ cup (125 mL) white port
- 1 [spoon] cider vinegar
- ½ cup (125 mL) water
- Salt and pepper

1. Cut the peppers into ¾ inch (2 cm) diamonds. Put them in the ActiFry pan with the onions and oil. Cook for 15 minutes.
2. Add garlic and cook 5 minutes. Season.
3. Add the turkey strips, port, water, cider vinegar and cook for about 15 minutes.

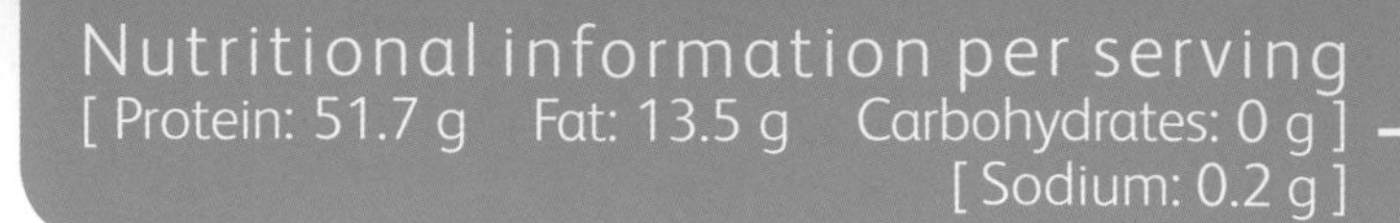

Nutritional information per serving
[Protein: 51.7 g Fat: 13.5 g Carbohydrates: 0 g]
[Sodium: 0.2 g]

Nutritious

Chicken drumsticks without the skin provide good quality protein with little fat. They work well for lunch with friends.

Spicy Chicken Drumsticks

Serves **6** • Preparation **5** min • Cooking **15** min

- 2 lb (1 kg) skinless chicken drumsticks
- 2 tbsp wine vinegar
- ½ tbsp Tabasco® sauce
- 3 tbsp olive oil
- Salt

1. Season the chicken drumsticks with vinegar, salt and Tabasco®. Marinate overnight.
2. Heat the oil in the ActiFry and add the drumsticks with the marinade. Cook for 15 minutes.

More flavours:

- You can make this same recipe using Dijon mustard instead of vinegar and Tabasco®.
- Try replacing the vinegar and Tabasco® with cumin and sesame oil.
- Try adding sesame seeds 5 minutes before the cooking is finished.

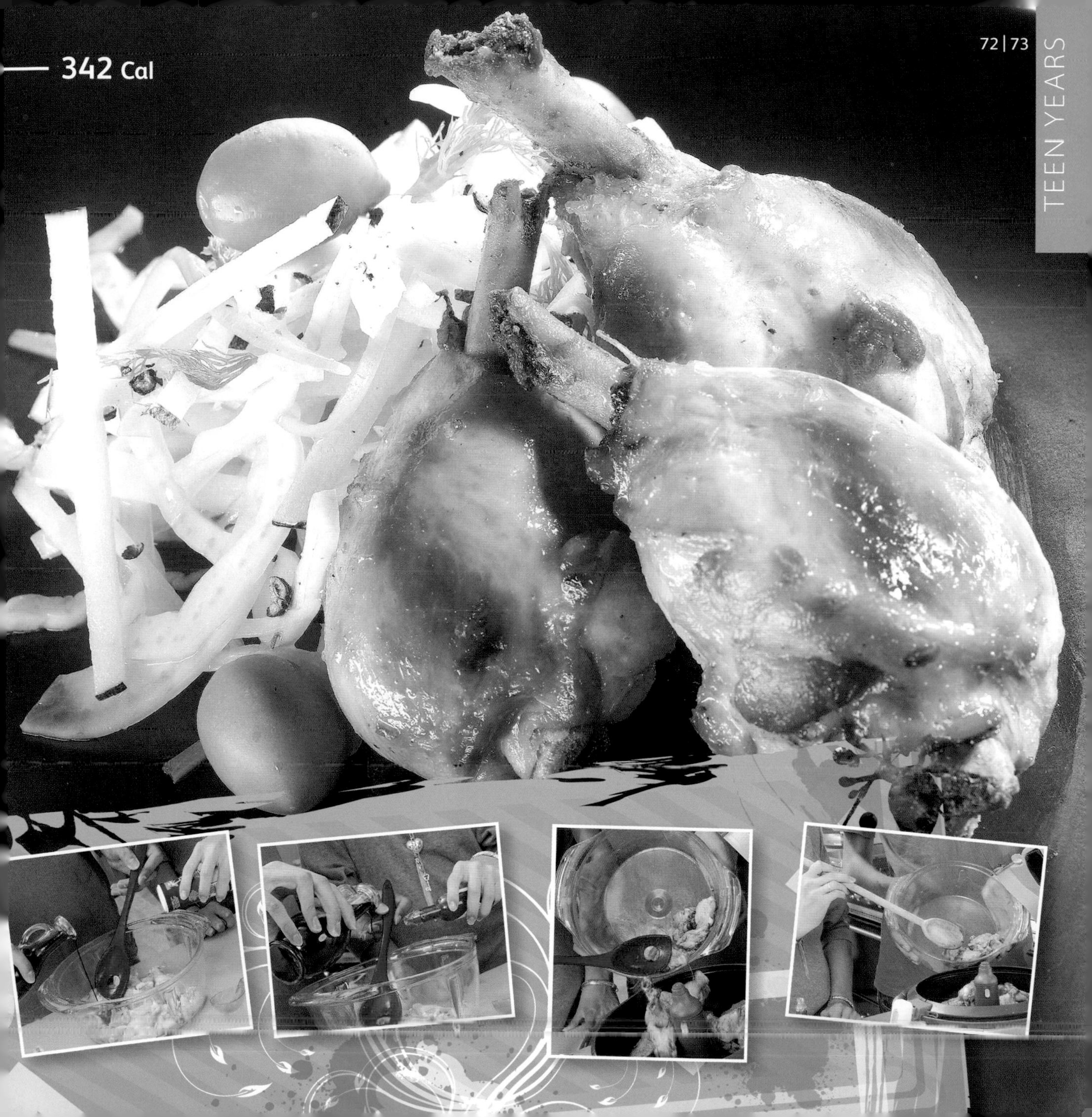

342 Cal

215 Cal
N.Y.

Nutritional information per serving
[Protein: 16.3 g Fat: 13 g Carbohydrates: 6.9 g]
[Sodium: 1.1 g]

This is a good way to rediscover mushrooms, a singular vegetable that is a good source of protein, vitamins and minerals with a woody taste all its own.

Mushroom Tarragon Chicken

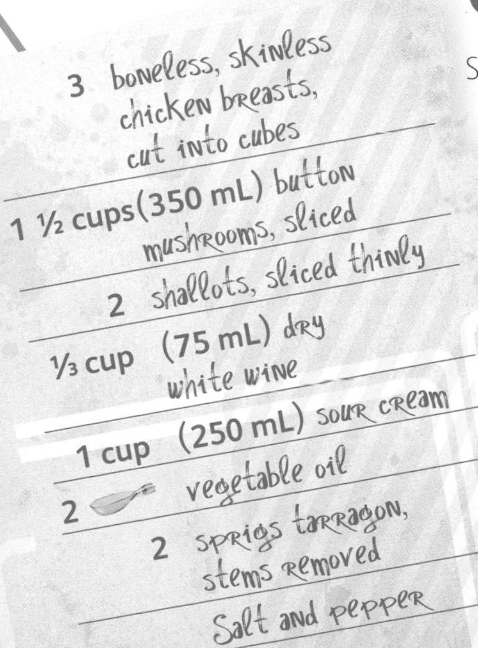

Serves **6** • Preparation **15** min • Cooking **12** min

1. Heat the ActiFry and add the seasoned chicken pieces. Cook for 3 minutes, and then add the shallots and the mushrooms. Continue cooking for 4 minutes.

2. Add the white wine and reduce before adding the cream. Boil for 5 minutes and then add the tarragon. Adjust the seasoning.

Nutritional information per serving
[Protein: 23 g Fat: 8.7 g Carbohydrates: 1.5 g]
[Sodium: 0 g]

Chicken Drumsticks with Garlic

Serves **6** • Preparation **10** min • Cooking **35** min

Nutritious

Choosing skinless chicken and cooking it in the ActiFry gives a recipe that is both low in fat and rich in good quality protein that is good for your muscles. Using garlic adds a little extra touch: it helps digestion, which you can improve even more by serving this dish with a mixed vegetables and whole grains.

- 2 lb (1 kg) skinless chicken drumsticks
- 4 cloves garlic, finely chopped
- 3 [spoon] vegetable oil
- Salt and pepper

1. Put the chicken drumsticks in the ActiFry with the vegetable oil and cook for 30 minutes.
2. Add the chopped garlic and cook for another 5 minutes. Season with salt and pepper.

Tip: Serve this dish with thyme-flavoured potatoes.

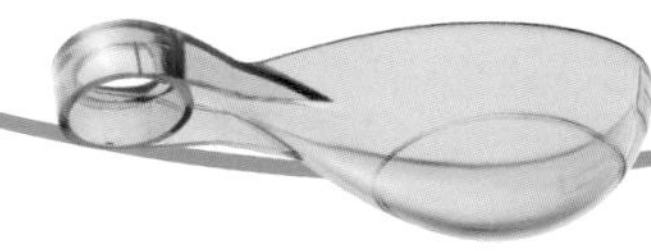

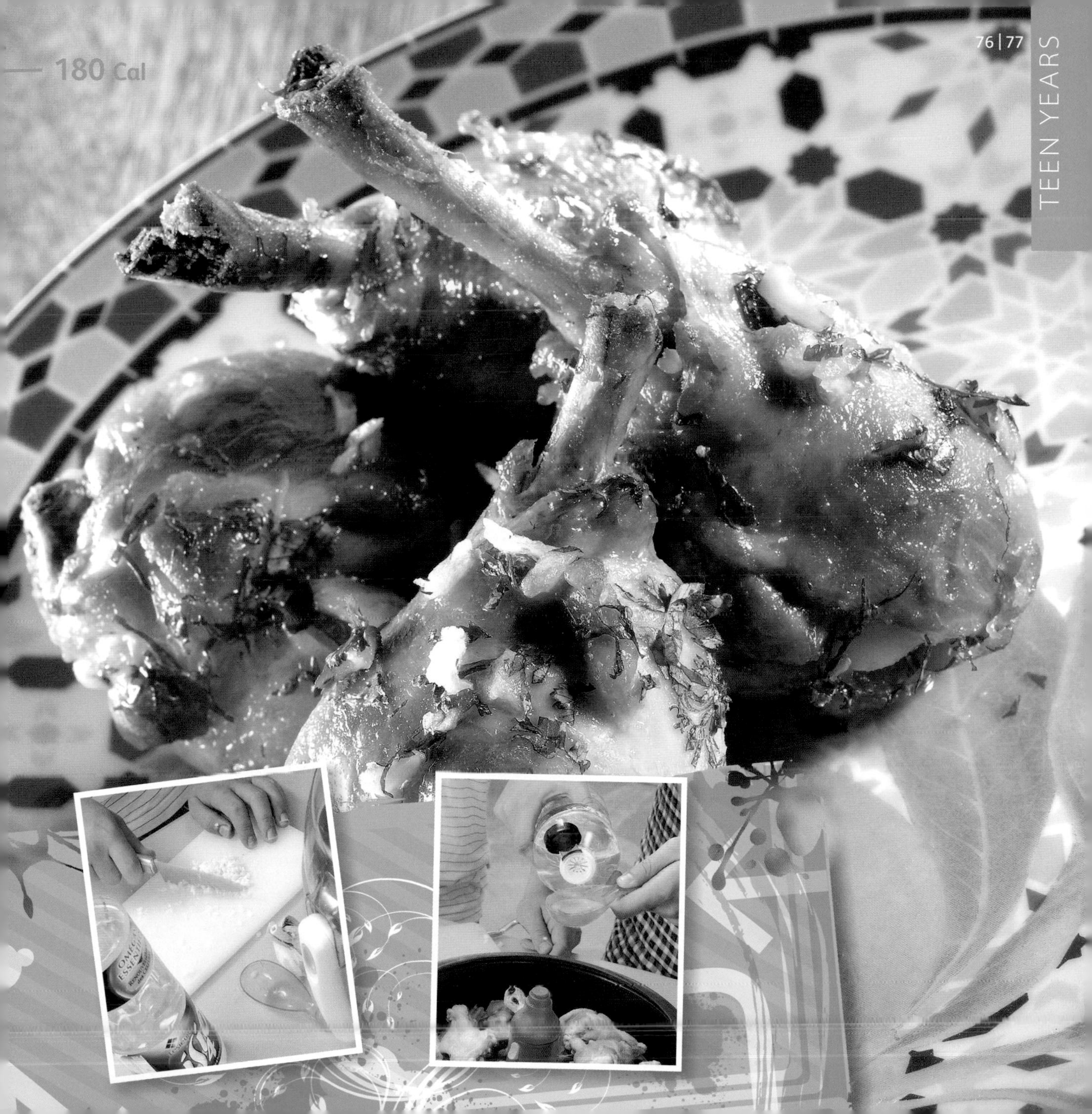

239 Cal

Nutritious

Prawns have a number of nutritional benefits. They are low in fat and have a lot of good quality protein, which is essential for healthy muscles. In addition, they have a lot of vitamins, in particular B12, which contributes to producing red blood cells, and B3, which gives off energy for your body's cells. They also have zinc, which is recognized for its antioxidant properties.

Nutritional information per serving
[Protein: 30.5 g Fat: 5.8 g Carbohydrates: 16.5 g]
[Sodium: 0.3 g]

Very Spicy Creole Prawns

Serves **6** • Preparation **15** min • Cooking **23** min

- 24 king prawns or shrimps, cooked and shelled
- 2 onions, sliced
- 2 green peppers, sliced
- 8 cloves garlic, finely chopped
- 3 (spoon) Cajun spice mix
- 1 ¼ cups (300 mL) tomato purée
- 2 (spoon) vegetable oil
- Salt and pepper

1. Heat the oil in the ActiFry for 2 minutes. Add the onions, peppers and garlic. Cook for 6 minutes.
2. Add the Cajun spice mix, the prawns and cook for another 5 minutes.
3. Finish off by adding the tomato purée and cook for another 10 minutes. Season to taste.

Nutritional information per serving
[Protein: 35.1 g Fat: 11 g Carbohydrates: 22.1 g]
[Sodium: 0.4 g]

Prawns with Tomatoes and Peas

Serves **6** • Preparation **30** min • Cooking **20** min

- 1 ¾ lb (875 g) cooked prawns, shelled
- 8 canned tomatoes, seeded and chopped
- 2 onions, sliced
- 20 basil leaves, chopped
- 4 [spoon] olive oil
- 3 cups (750 mL) peas
- Salt and pepper

1 Put the prawns and the onion slices in the ActiFry. Pour in the oil and cook for 5 minutes.

2 Add the chopped tomatoes, the basil leaves and the peas. Season and cook for 15 minutes. Adjust the seasoning.

328 Cal

Nutritious

This recipe provides excellent quality protein from the prawns, which also have the advantage of being low in fat. Here, by using the ActiFry, you get the most out of the flavours of the prawns and basil, and you only add a little fat. In addition, the tomatoes contain lycopene, which is an antioxidant, and the peas are complex carbohydrates that help you feel full.

216 Cal

Nutritional information per serving
[Protein: 11.2 g Fat: 9.3 g Carbohydrates: 23.5 g]
[Sodium: 0.1 g]

Nutritious

Eggs have very interesting nutritional properties: they contain very good quality protein needed for healthy muscles, along with vitamin A and E, and antioxidant zinc, not to mention vitamin D to fix calcium to the bones. Potatoes provide excellent complex carbohydrates to make you feel full.

ActiFried Scrambled Tortilla

Serves **6** • Preparation **10** min • Cooking **34** min

- 4 potatoes, peeled and washed
- 1 onion
- 8 eggs
- 1 [spoon] olive oil
- Salt and pepper

1. Cut the potatoes into cubes. Put them in the ActiFry. Pour in the oil and cook for 20 minutes.
2. Add the onion and cook for 10 more minutes.
3. Add the beaten eggs and cook for 4 minutes. Season. Serve the scrambled tortilla on a plate.

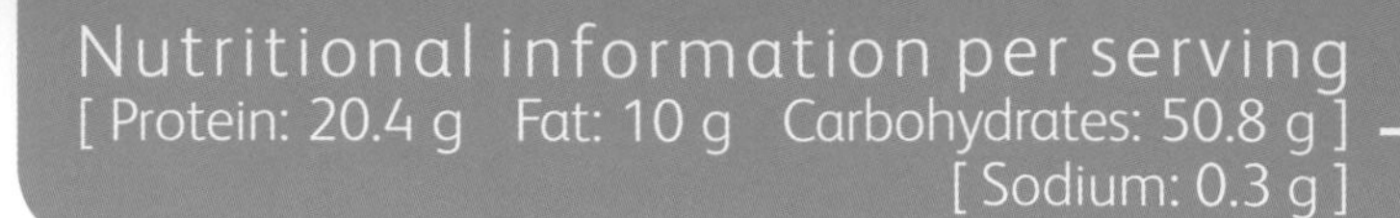

Nutritional information per serving
[Protein: 20.4 g Fat: 10 g Carbohydrates: 50.8 g]

[Sodium: 0.3 g]

✚ Nutritious

With ActiFry, it is easy to make perfectly balanced fried rice. This recipe contains both good quality proteins and complex carbohydrates. Do not hesitate to serve it with a green salad seasoned with walnut oil.

Fried Rice

Serves **6** • Preparation **35** min • Cooking **15-20** min

- 3 Chinese or dried pork sausages
- 18 cooked prawns or shrimps
- 5 peas
- 4 ½ cups (1.125 L) cooked rice
- 3 eggs, beaten
- 2 onions, chopped
- 1 soya oil
- 2 water
- Salt and pepper

1. Put the onions and oil in the ActiFry and cook until soft for 5 minutes.
2. Add the diced sausage and cook for 5 minutes. Add the peas, eggs and prawns. Continue cooking for 5 minutes.
3. Add the cooked rice. Pour in a little cold water and cook for 5 to 10 additional minutes. Adjust the seasoning and serve.

382 Cal

286 Cal
Tip: You can use cocoa powder or Nutella® instead of cocoa nibs.

Nutritional information per serving
[Protein: 6.5 g   Fat: 6.6 g   Carbohydrates: 31.6 g]
[Sodium: 0.01 g]

Nutritious

Brick pastry contains very little fat and is an excellent ingredient to use to make light, flaky desserts. Cocoa nibs contain a good quantity of flavonoids, which are antioxidants.

ActiFried Mini Banana and Cocoa Nib Packets

Serves **6** • Preparation **30** min • Cooking **10** min

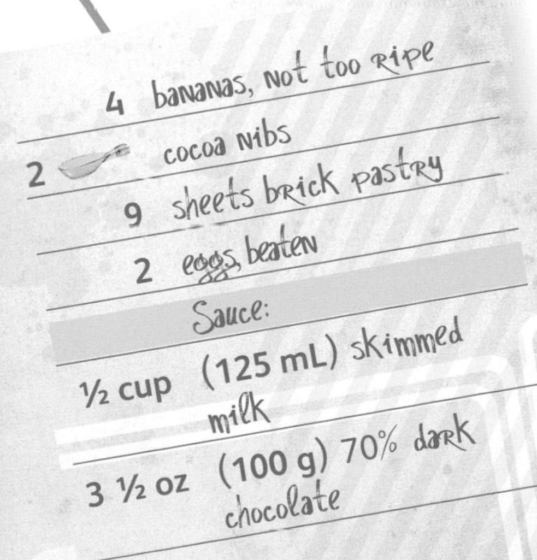

4 bananas, not too ripe
2 [spoon] cocoa nibs
9 sheets brick pastry
2 eggs, beaten

Sauce:
½ cup (125 mL) skimmed milk
3 ½ oz (100 g) 70% dark chocolate

1. Cut the bananas into slices ½ inch (1 cm) thick. Cut the brick pastry sheets in four.
2. Put a little bit of cocoa nibs in the centre of each piece of brick pastry and top with a banana slice. Close up the packet by folding over the two opposing sides and then the two other sides and brush with beaten egg to seal. Put the packets in the ActiFry, sealed side down, and cook for 10 minutes.
3. Meanwhile, heat the milk and add the chocolate. Blend the sauce until smooth.

Nutritional information per serving
[Protein: 2 g Fat: 8 g Carbohydrates: 33.1 g]
[Sodium: 0 g]

+ Nutritious

This apple and hazelnut dessert is a good source of complex carbohydrates and essential fatty acids.

Apples, Hazelnuts and Popcorn

Serves **6** • Preparation **20** min • Cooking **30** min

- 6 Golden Delicious apples
- 4 cups (1 L) popcorn
- ⅓ cup (75 mL) whole, shelled hazelnuts
- 3 [spoon] liquid caramel or caramel sauce

1 Peel the apples and cut into wedges to remove the seeds and then cut into ½ inch (1 cm) cubes.

2 Put the apples in the ActiFry and pour the caramel over them evenly. Cook for 25 minutes.

3 Add the hazelnuts and the popcorn, then cook for another 5 minutes.

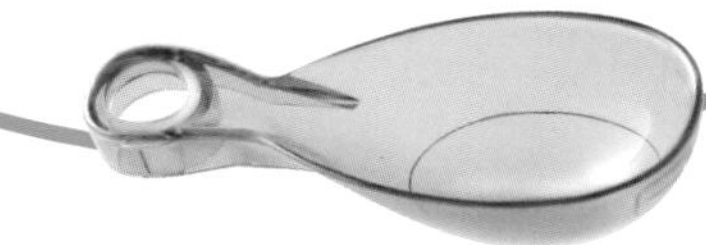

199 Cal

Family Reunion

Sharing and enjoyment...

Nutritional information per serving
[Protein: 5.3 g   Fat: 6.5 g   Carbohydrates: 66.4 g]
[Sodium: 0.3 g]

Less fat, but more colour and flavour. That's proof that a balanced diet can taste good!

Paprika Fries

Serves **6** • Preparation **15** min • Cooking **45** min

- **3 lb** (**1.5 kg**) potatoes, peeled and washed
- 1 quality vegetable oil
- 2 hazelnut oil
- 2 paprika

1 Cut the potatoes into fries ½ inch (1 cm) thick. Wash the cut fries well, drain and dry carefully.

2 Mix the vegetable oil, hazelnut oil and paprika together in a bowl.

3 Put the chips in the ActiFry pan and pour this mixture evenly over them. Cook for 45 minutes.

— 256 Cal

425 Cal

Nutritional information per serving
[Protein: 39.5 g Fat: 26 g Carbohydrates: 4.8 g]
[Sodium: 0.1 g]

Nutritious

The majority of the fat in the recipe, from the lamb and the hazelnut oil, contains fatty acids that contribute to a healthy cardiovascular system. This recipe is rich in fat, which means that is should be saved for special occasions.

Lamb Sautéed with Hazelnuts

Serves **6** • Preparation **15** min • Cooking **20** min

- **2 lb** (**1 kg**) lamb (shoulder or saddle), boneless, cut into strips 1 inch x ½ inch (2.5 cm x 1 cm)
- **2** [spoon] hazelnut oil
- **1 cup** (**250 mL**) toasted hazelnuts
- **½ cup** (**125 mL**) water
- **⅔ cup** (**150 mL**) dry white wine
- Salt and pepper

Sauce:

- **2** eggs
- **6** lemons, juiced

1. Put the lamb in the ActiFry pan, pour in the oil and cook for 7 minutes.
2. Season with salt and pepper, add the glass of water and the glass of white wine. Cook for 13 minutes.
3. Add the hazelnuts, which you first toasted to remove the skin.

Lemon sauce:

1. Beat the eggs and whisk in the lemon juice.
2. Add a little bit of the cooking juices and whisk well.

Nutritional information per serving
[Protein: 35.5 g Fat: 15.1 g Carbohydrates: 16.3 g]
[Sodium: 0.2 g]

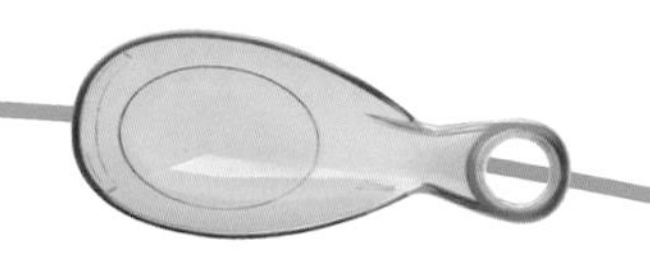

2 lb	(1 kg) lamb shoulder, cubed
1 oz	(30 g) fresh gingerroot, sliced
⅓ cup	(75 mL) pilled black olives
3	salt-preserved lemons
3	cloves garlic, sliced thinly
1	bunch coriander leaves (cilantro), chopped
½ cup	(125 mL) bunch parsley, finely chopped
2	pinches ground ginger
4	saffron threads
2	cornflour (cornstarch)
⅔ cup	(150 mL) dry white wine
2	olive oil
	Salt and pepper

Lamb Tajine with Preserved Lemons and Black Olives

Serves **6** • Preparation **25** min • Cooking **30** min

1. Remove the pulp from the preserved lemons and slice the zest thinly. Mix the cornflour and saffron with ⅔ cup (150 mL) water and the wine.
2. Put the oil, gingerroot, garlic and onion in the ActiFry and cook for 5 minutes. Add the meat and continue cooking for another 10 minutes.
3. Add the remaining ingredients and cook yet another 10 to 15 minutes to taste. Season.

Tip: Sprinkle with herbs right before serving.

369 Cal

Nutritious

It is important to underline that although lamb is a fatty meat, it has a number of nutritional benefits: it contains the fatty acid omega-9, which contributes to balancing out lipid intake, and it also has iron, zinc, phosphorus and B vitamins. That is why, for this recipe, we recommend you choose a lean cut, such as the shoulder with fat removed. Serve this flavourful dish with steamed vegetables, and it fits perfectly in a balanced diet.

362 Cal

Nutritional information per serving
[Protein: 33.4 g Fat: 12.3 g Carbohydrates: 30.3 g]
[Sodium: 0.9 g]

Nutritious

This recipe is a perfect marriage of animal protein, found in the beef, and plant protein, found the red beans. Protein is essential for our muscles to function properly. This dish also provides you with fibre for good digestion and lycopene, which is an antioxidant found in tomatoes.

Beef with Beans

Serves **6** • Preparation **10** min • Cooking **14** min

- **1 ½ lb** (**750 g**) lean steak
- **1** (spoon) olive oil
- **1** large onion, sliced
- **2 ½ cups** (**625 mL**) canned diced tomatoe w/ juce
- **1 ¼ cups** (**300 mL**) sodium reduced beef broth
- **1** (spoon) fresh thyme
- **3 cups** (**750 mL**) canned red kidney beans, rinsed and drained
- Salt and pepper

1 Trim the fat from the meat and cut into thin strips. Add the oil and onions to the ActiFry pan and cook for 5 minutes. Add the meat and continue cooking for 5 minutes.

2 Add the tomatoes and their juice, the stock, the thyme and the beans and cook for 4 minutes. Season with black pepper.

Tip: Serve with tortillas or nachos.

Nutritional information per serving
[Protein: 22.4 g Fat: 12.2 g Carbohydrates: 6.2 g]
[Sodium: 0.2 g]

Nutritious

Serve this protein-rich and vegetable-filled sauce with pasta, rice or polenta to have a complete, nutritionally balanced meal that could end with a dairy product or a piece of fruit.

Bolognaise Sauce

Serves **6** • Preparation **10** min • Cooking **50** min

1 ¼ lb	**(625 g)** extra lean ground beef
1	onion, finely chopped
½ cup	**(125 mL)** red wine
1 lb	**(500 g)** tomatoes, peeled
3	olive oil
	Salt and pepper

1 Heat the oil in the ActiFry, add the onion and cook for 5 minutes. Add the minced meat, season and cook for another 10 minutes.

2 Pour in the red wine and continue cooking for 5 minutes.

3 Blend the peeled tomatoes in a food processor and add. Cook for 30 minutes.

Tip: Serve with macaroni.

237 Cal

389 Cal

Nutritional information per serving
[Protein: 34.3 g Fat: 17.4 g Carbohydrates: 11.9 g]
[Sodium: 0.07 g]

Nutritious

Rabbit is particularly interesting nutritionally speaking: it has little fat, and contains iron and vitamin B12 to fight anaemia, as well as protein for the muscular system.

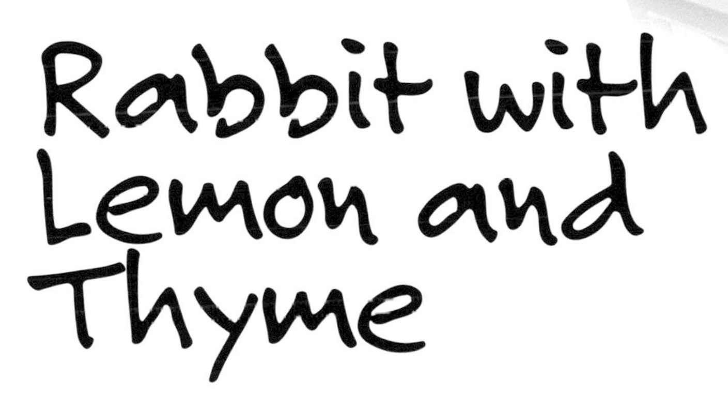

Rabbit with Lemon and Thyme

Serves **6** • Preparation **20** min • Cooking **25** min

- **2 lb** (**1 kg**) saddle of rabbit, cut into small pieces
- 4 spoons olive oil
- 2 large onions, sliced
- 4 lemons, juiced
- **1 cup** (**250 mL**) dry white wine
- **½ cup** (**125 mL**) water
- **½ cup** (**125 mL**) parsley
- 2 sprigs fresh thyme
- Salt and white pepper

1. Cook the onion with 2 spoons of olive oil for 5 minutes.
2. Add the rabbit pieces and the remaining olive oil, along with the thyme, dry white wine, lemon juice and water. Season and cook for 20 minutes.
3. Just before serving, sprinkle with chopped parsley and thyme.

Tip: Serve this dish with steamed potatoes.

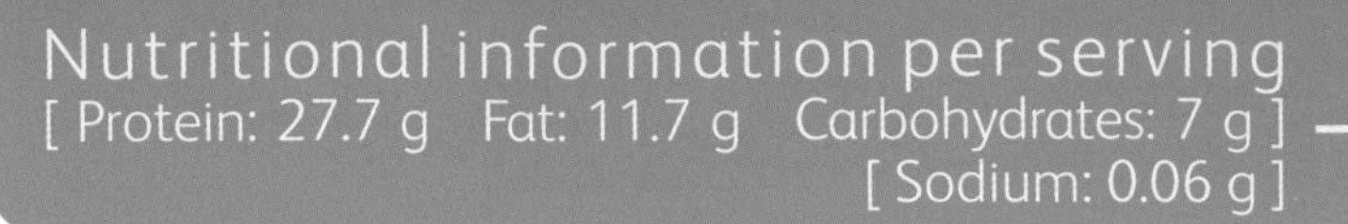

Nutritional information per serving
[Protein: 27.7 g Fat: 11.7 g Carbohydrates: 7 g]
[Sodium: 0.06 g]

Nutritious

Rabbit is particularly interesting nutritionally speaking: it has little fat, and contains iron and vitamin B12 to fight anaemia, as well as protein for the muscular system.

Spicy Rabbit

Serves **6** • Preparation **15** min • Cooking **45** min

- **1** rabbit, weighing 3 lb (1.5 kg), cut into small pieces
- **1** red pepper
- **⅔ cup** (**150 mL**) dry white wine
- **2** cloves garlic, finely chopped
- **1** sliced onion
- **2** olive oil
- **½** ground Espellette or other medium chilli pepper
- Salt and pepper

1. Heat the oil in the ActiFry. Season the rabbit and add the ActiFry. Cook for 5 minutes.
2. Add the pepper, garlic, onion and chilli pepper. Continue cooking for 15 minutes.
3. Add the white wine and cook for another 25 minutes.

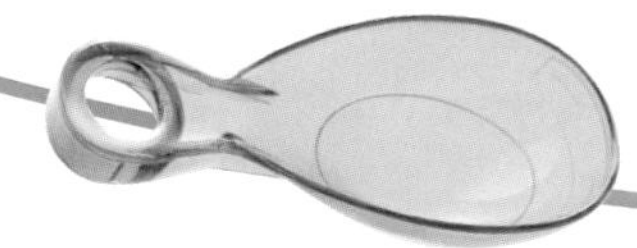

266 Cal

323 Cal

Nutritional information per serving
[Protein: 35.4 g Fat: 13.6 g Carbohydrates: 3.8 g]
[Sodium: 0.09 g]

✚ Nutritious

This recipe is rich in good quality protein. In addition, the olive oil contains monounsaturated fatty acids, which contribute to cardiovascular function.

Alentejo-style Pork Tenderloin

Serves **6** • Preparation **15** min • Cooking **20** min

- **2 lb** (**1 kg**) pork tenderloin, cut into cubes
- **1** onion, sliced
- **1 ¼ cup** (**300 mL**) dry white wine
- **3** [spoon] olive oil
- Paprika to taste
- Salt and pepper

1 Put the oil and onions in the ActiFry and brown for 5 minutes.

2 Add the meat, salt, pepper and paprika. Pour in the white wine and cook for 15 minutes.

Tip: Serve with chips made in the ActiFry.

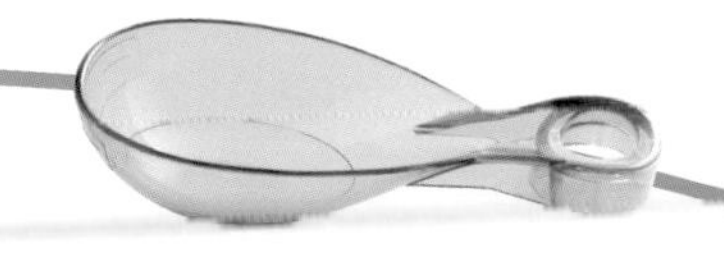

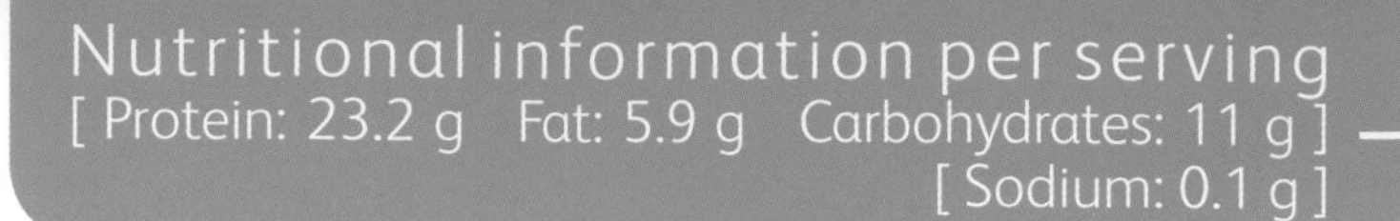

Nutritional information per serving
[Protein: 23.2 g Fat: 5.9 g Carbohydrates: 11 g]

[Sodium: 0.1 g]

Chicken Tikka Masala

Serves **6** • Preparation **15** min • Cooking **30** min

Nutritious

Usually chicken masala usually brings to mind a fatty dish made with ghee (butter) and cream. This lower fat version uses vegetable oil instead of butter and low fat yoghurt for a healthier version.

- **1 lb** (**500 g**) boneless skinless chicken breasts, cut into 2 cm pieces
- **100 g** Tikka Masala curry paste
- **2 pots** (**150 g size**) natural low fat yoghurt
- **1** [spoon] vegetable oil
- **1** large onion, finely chopped
- **390 g** can premium chopped tomatoes
- **⅔ cup** (**150 mL**) water
- **½** teaspoon sugar
- **2** teaspoons fresh lemon juice
- **1** bunch coriander leaves, chopped

1 In a large bowl mix Tikka masala paste with 3 tablespoons yoghurt. Add the chicken, stir to coat then cover. Leave to marinate in the fridge for at least 2 hours or overnight if you have time.

2 Heat the oil in ActiFry for 2 minutes, add the onion and cook for 5 mintues. Add the marinated chicken and cook for another 10 minutes.

3 Add the chopped tomatoes and water. Cook for another 10 minutes. Add the yoghurt, sugar and lemon juice. Stir well with a wooden spoon and cook for another 5 minutes. Serve hot sprinkled with chopped coriander and accompanied by basmati rice or naan bread.

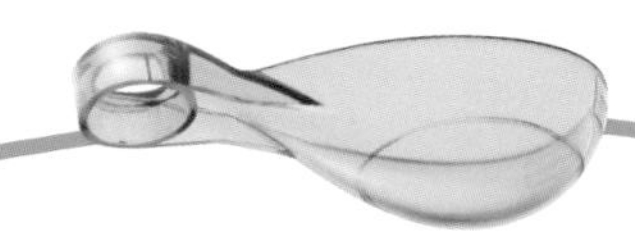

191 Cal

226 Cal

Nutritional information per serving
[Protein: 28 g Fat: 7 g Carbohydrates: 14 g]
[Sodium: 0.1 g]

Nutritious

The word "kebab" usually brings to mind a fatty dish. In this version, the choice of veal tenderloin and only a small amount of oil make it perfectly balanced and light.

ActiFried Kebab

Serves **6** • Preparation **15** min • Cooking **27** min

- **1 ½ lb** **(750 g)** veal fillet
- **2** lemons, juiced
- **2** ground red chilli
- **2 cups** **(500 mL)** tomato sauce or passata
- **2** cloves garlic, finely chopped
- **1** onion, finely chopped
- **1** olive oil
- **⅓ cup** **(75 mL)** ground cumin
- Salt

1. Cut the veal fillet into cubes and mix with the lemon, ground cumin and ground red chilli.
2. Cook the garlic and onion with the oil for 5 minutes. Then add the marinated veal and cook for another 15 minutes.
3. Add the tomato sauce and cook for another 7 minutes. Serve hot.

Nutritional information per serving
[Protein: 36.4 g Fat: 16.9 g Carbohydrates: 20.2 g]
[Sodium: 0.9 g]

Nutritious

This recipe combines the good quality protein found in the veal, which is good for the muscles, and essential fatty acids for a healthy cardiovascular system.

Veal Sauté with Olives

Serves **6** • Preparation **10** min • Cooking **30** min

- **2 lb** (**1 kg**) veal fillet cut into ½ inch (1 cm) by 1 inch (2.5 cm) strips
- **⅔ cup** (**150 mL**) all-purpose flour
- **3 cups** (**750 mL**) green onions finely chopped
- **4** olive oil
- **2 cups** (**500 mL**) sodium-reduced chicken broth
- **1** handful parsley, finely chopped
- **20** olives
- Salt and pepper

1 Put the onions in the ActiFry with the oil and brown for 5 minutes.

2 Add the veal stock and the olives and cook another 5 minutes.

3 Mix the veal, flour and seasoning in a bowl. Pour into the ActiFry and cook for 20 minutes.

Tip: Serve with fresh pasta.

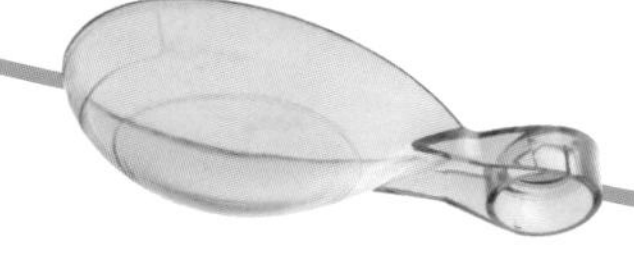

381 Cal

251 Cal

Nutritional information per serving
[Protein: 31.4 g Fat: 7.8 g Carbohydrates: 15 g]
[Sodium: 2.5 g]

Nutritious

Poultry has "good fat", because it is mainly monounsaturated and polyunsaturated, which contributes to the cardiovascular system. In addition, pineapple contains a number of minerals and vitamins.

Pineapple Chicken

Serves **6** • Preparation **15** min • Cooking **18** min

- **2 lb** (**1 kg**) boneless chicken cut into thin strips (½ inch by 1 inch)
- **2 cups** (**500 mL**) pineapple, cut into cubes
- 3 soya sauce
- 3 pineapple juice
- 1.5 cornflour (cornstarch) + 1 tbsp (15 mL)
- 1 ground ginger
- 1 mild curry powder
- 3 quality vegetable oil
- **1 cup** (**250 mL**) water
- Salt and pepper

1. In a bowl, mix the chicken strips with the cornflour, salt and pepper to coat them. Put them in the ActiFry pan and pour in the vegetable oil. Cook for 8 minutes.
2. Stop the ActiFry, add the ground ginger, curry powder and pineapples and mix. Marinate for 5 minutes. Add the soya sauce and water. Mix 1 tablespoon of cornflour with the pineapple juice and add to the ActiFry.
3. Cook for another 5 minutes.

Tip: Serve with basmati rice or wild rice.

Nutritional information per serving
[Protein: 25.3 g   Fat: 7.9 g   Carbohydrates: 14.8 g]
[Sodium: 0.2 g]

Nutritious

Chicken is low in fat and provides good quality protein. This recipe is complete with plant protein from the peas.

Chicken
with Peas and Carrots

Serves **6** • Preparation **15** min • Cooking **20** min

1 ¼ lb	(**625 g**) skinless, boneless chicken, sliced
2 cups	(**500 mL**) frozen peas
2 cups	(**500 mL**) frozen baby carrots
1	onion, finely chopped
2	tomato paste mixed with 1 cup (250 mL) water
2	olive oil
	Salt and pepper

1 Put the oil and chicken in the ActiFry and cook for 5 minutes. Add the onion and cook another 5 minutes.

2 Add the peas, carrots and tomato sauce. Cook for an additional 10 minutes. Season with salt and pepper.

— 230 Cal

304 Cal

Nutritional information per serving
[Protein: 35.1 g Fat: 13.1 g Carbohydrates: 11 g]
[Sodium: 0.25 g]

Nutritious

King prawns have very few calories and contain primarily good quality protein essential to strong muscles, along with B vitamins.

Provence-style King Prawns

Serves **6** • Preparation **20** min • Cooking **15** min

- **2 lb** (**1 kg**) uncooked king prawns or shrimps, shelled
- **2** onions, sliced
- **6** cloves garlic, finely chopped
- **½ cup** (**125 mL**) bunch parsley, finely chopped
- **5** [spoon] olive oil
- **2** lemons
- Salt and pepper

1. Marinate the prawns for 15 minutes with the garlic, onion, parsley and oil. Season with salt and pepper.
2. Put the prawns and the marinade in the ActiFry for 15 minutes. You can eat the prawns when they turn a deep orange colour.
3. Serve with lemon wedges.

Tip: It could be useful to put small bowls of warm water with lemon on the table for each person, so they can rinse their fingers.

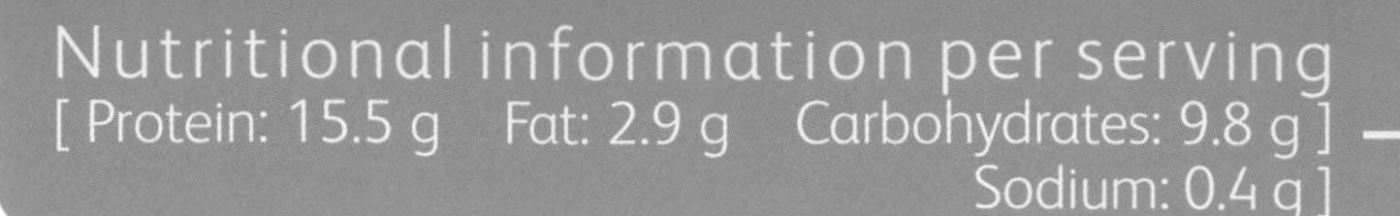

Nutritional information per serving
[Protein: 15.5 g Fat: 2.9 g Carbohydrates: 9.8 g]
Sodium: 0.4 g]

Nutritious

Mussels are an excellent source of protein and contain omega-3 fatty acids, which protect the cardiovascular system. In addition, they are a goldmine of essential nutrients such as phosphorus, iron, zinc, selenium, copper, and vitamins B1, B2, B12, B3, and B9. Tomatoes contain lycopene, a red pigment with antioxidant properties. Serve this dish with a small portion of rice and a dash of olive oil, and it will be perfectly well balanced.

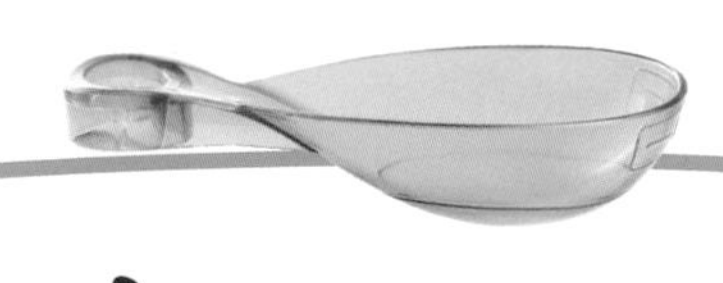

Marinière Mussels with Cherry Tomatoes and Basil

Serves **6** • Preparation **20** min • Cooking **29** min

6 lb	**(3 kg)** mussels
1 ¼ lb	**(625 g)** cherry tomatoes
1	onion, finely chopped
1 ¼ cup	**(300 mL)** dry white wine
3	cloves garlic
1	bunch fresh basil
	Salt and pepper

1 Clean the mussels and the cherry tomatoes. You will cook the mussels in three batches.

2 Cook the onions, cherry tomatoes, garlic and white wine together in the ActiFry for 8 minutes. Add the mussels, salt and pepper and cook another 7 minutes.

3 Remove the first batch of mussels and sprinkle with basil. Eat them while you get another batch cooking.

166 Cal

144 Cal

Nutritional information per serving
[Protein: 4.7 g Fat: 6.7 g Carbohydrates: 15.5 g]
[Sodium: 0.02 g]

Nutritious

This recipe goes ideally with roast meat and fish. It is full of vegetables (2 of the 5 recommended daily portions) and vitamins and minerals. To these qualities, you can add a good supply of antioxidants found in the olive oil.

Mediterranean Vegetable Stir-fry

Serves **6** • Preparation **10** min • Cooking **30** min

2	zucchinis
4 cups	(**1 L**) sliced button mushrooms
1	eggplant
1	red pepper
½	green pepper
⅔ cup	(**150 mL**) dry white wine
3	cloves garlic
	A few sprigs of parsley
3	olive oil
	Salt and pepper

1 Cut the zucchinis and eggplant into cubes. Slice the mushrooms. Cut the peppers into thin strips.

2 Put the eggplant, zucchini, peppers and mushrooms in the ActiFry. Pour in the oil and cook for 15 minutes.

3 Crush the garlic and the parsley. Add the white wine. Season and continue cooking for another 15 minutes.

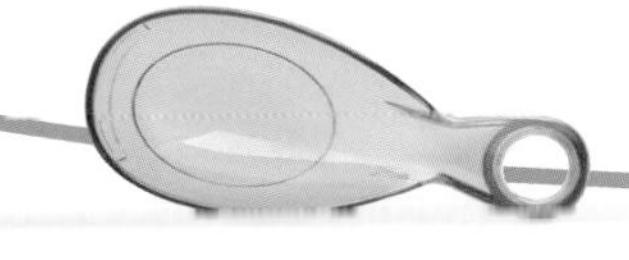

Nutritional information per serving
[Protein: 23.8 g Fat: 18.2 g Carbohydrates : 63.3 g]
[Sodium: 1.9 g]

Nutritious

Rice provides slowly absorbed complex carbohydrates that progressively give off their energy so that you do not feel hungry and crave food between meals. The parmesan in the recipe helps to meet your calcium needs to have strong bones. Special risotto rice contains plant proteins, which along with those from the parmesan, make this an ideal dish to serve at dinner.

Sun-dried Tomato and Scallion Risotto

Serves **6** • Preparation **10** min • Cooking **30** min

- **1 ½ cups (375 mL)** special risotto rice or arborio
- **3 tbs (45 mL)** butter
- **2 ⅓ cups (575 mL)** parmesan cheese
- **3 ¼ cups (800 mL)** vegetable broth
- **18** sun-dried tomatoes in oil, diced
- **8** scallions, thinly sliced
- Salt and pepper

1. Heat the butter for 3 minutes in the ActiFry, then add the rice and cook for 2 minutes.
2. Add the stock and cook for 25 minutes.
3. Just before serving, add the parmesan, tomatoes and scallions, then season with salt and pepper.

500 Cal

497 Cal

Nutritional information per serving
[Protein: 32.4 g   Fat: 16.5 g   Carbohydrates: 44.9 g]
[Sodium: 1.3 g]

Nutritious

This risotto is well balanced and complete. It contains good protein for your muscles, iodine and complex carbohydrates so you feel satiated. It is ideal with a starter of raw vegetables and with a piece of fruit to complete the meal with vitamins and fibre.

Curry Risotto

Serves **6** • Preparation **15** min • Cooking **32** min

- **1 ½ cups** (**375 mL**) uncooked rice
- **½ cup** (**125 mL**) chopped onion
- **36** cooked prawns, shelleds
- **½ tsp** (**2 mL**) curry powder
- **2 tbsp** (**30 mL**) butter
- **1 cup** (**250 mL**) dry white wine
- **½ cup** (**125 mL**) finely chopped coriander (cilantro)
- **2 ⅓ cups** (**575 mL**) grated parmesan cheese
- **3 cups** (**750 mL**) reduced sodium chicken broth

1. Melt the butter in the ActiFry. Add the onion and cook for 5 minutes. Add the rice, curry powder and brown for 2 minutes. Pour in the white wine and reduce.
2. Add the stock and cook for 25 minutes. Then add the parmesan, prawns and coriander leaves. Season to taste.
3. The risotto should be creamy when it is finished cooking.

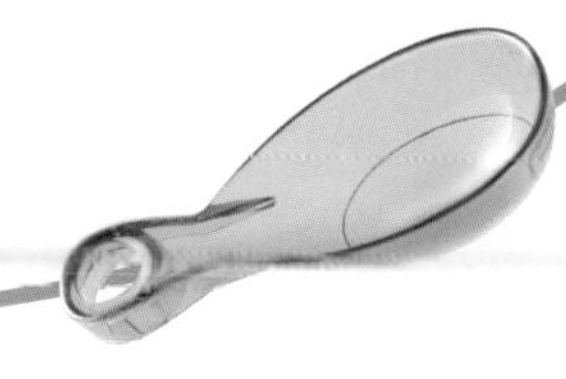

Nutritional information per serving
[Protein: 24.6 g Fat: 14.7 g Carbohydrates: 32.8 g]
[Sodium: 0.2 g]

Spanish-style ActiFried Tofu

Serves **6** • Preparation **15** min • Cooking **35** min

1 ½ lb	(**750 g**) firm, plain tofu
1	large green pepper diced
1	large tomato chopped
2 cups	(**500 mL**) cooked basmati rice
1 ½ oz	(**40 g**) chorizo, cut into thin slices
⅓ cup	pitted black olives
1 (spoon)	tomato paste or purée
1	large onion, finely chopped
	Salt and pepper

1 Put the onions and peppers in the ActiFry and cook for 10 minutes.

2 Add the chorizo. Cook for 10 minutes. Add the tomato paste, chopped tomatoes and olives. Cook for another 5 minutes.

3 Drain the tofu, cut into ½ inch (1 cm) cubes and add to the ActiFry. Cook 5 minutes.

4 Add the rice and cook for 5 more minutes. Season to taste.

345 Cal

Nutritious

Unlike other plant protein, the soya protein found in tofu is excellent for the body, because it contains all the amino acids you need. You will get everything you need in this perfectly balanced paëlla. The peppers and tomato contain vitamin C, flavonoids and carotenoids, which are antioxidants. And the basmati rice contains complex carbohydrates that increase your feeling of fullness so you can make it to the following meal without craving snacks.

178 Cal

Nutritional information per serving
[Protein: 5.5 g Fat: 13.8 g Carbohydrates: 9.9 g]
[Sodium: 0.01 g]

Nutritious

This is an original way to rediscover green beans. You can enjoy new flavours while you benefit from their numerous nutritional properties: antioxidant vitamin A, vitamin C for vitality, and B9 for its contribution to the immune system, not to mention the digestive properties of sage.

Green Beans with Fresh Sage and Almonds

Serves **6** • Preparation **5** min • Cooking **20** min

- **2 lb** (**1 kg**) green beans trimmed
- **⅓ cup** (**75 mL**) whole or flaked almonds
- **¼ cup** (**50 mL**) finely chopped fresh sage
- **⅔ cup** (**150 mL**) 35 % whipping cream
- **1** [spoon] oil
- **⅔ cup** (**150 mL**) water
- Salt and pepper

1 Pour the oil in the ActiFry pan and cook the beans for about 10 minutes with water and the sage.

2 Add the almonds and cream. Cook for an additional 10 minutes. Season with salt and pepper to taste.

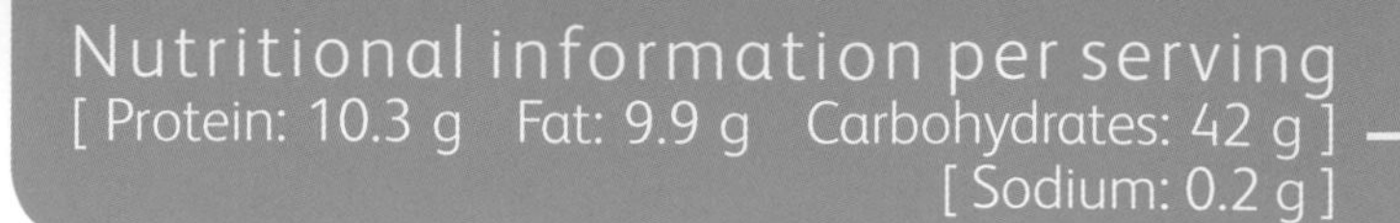

Italian-style Vegetables

Serves **6** • Preparation **20** min • Cooking **40** min

Nutritious

This dish of Italian-style vegetables fits perfectly into a Mediterranean diet and provides a complete, well-balanced meal. It contains one of your five recommended daily portions of fruit and vegetables, with a good quantity of fibre and vitamins.

- **2** eggplants, cut into small cubes
- **3 ½ cups (875 mL)** baby green beans, trimmed and chopped
- **3** yellow peppers, grilled, peeled, seeded and cut into strips
- **1** small romanesco (or regular) cauliflower
- **2** onions, sliced
- **2** cloves garlic, crushed
- **1 cup (250 mL)** pitted black olives, chopped
- **3** (spoons) olive oil
- **1 cup (250 mL)** fresh basil, stems removed and chopped
- Salt and pepper

1. Put the onions, eggplant, peppers and oil in the ActiFry. Cook for 10 minutes.
2. Add the beans, romanesco and crushed garlic. Season and add 1½ cups (375 mL) of water. Cook for another 30 minutes.
3. Add the olives and basil. Season with salt and pepper.

Tip: Serve with fresh pasta.

283 Cal

Nutritious

We do not use sweet potatoes very often in our culinary tradition, which is too bad. Like beetroots and pumpkins, they contain a number of antioxidant pigments that help prevent cell ageing. These vegetables also contain large amounts of food fibre, which helps digestion and regulates cholesterol levels. Olive oil contains vitamin E, an antioxidant, and the fatty acid omega-9, which protects the cardiovascular system.

Nutritional information per serving
[Protein: 6.5 g Fat: 6.5 g Carbohydrates: 57.7 g]
[Sodium: 0.1 g]

Grated Vegetable Terrine with Lemon and Chives

Serves **6** • Preparation **30** • Cooking **30** min each vegetable

1 ½ lb	**(750 g)** potatoes, peeled and grated
1 ½ lb	**(750 g)** sweet potatoes, peeled and grated
1 ¼ lb	**(625 g)** pumpkin, peeled and grated
½ lb	**(250 g)** cooked beetroot, grated
1	lemon, juiced
½ cup	**(125 mL)** chopped chives
3 (spoons)	olive oil
	Salt and pepper

1 Add a spoon of oil to the grated potatoes, one to the grated pumpkin and one to the grated sweet potatoes. Season each of the grated vegetables. Put the grated potatoes in the ActiFry and cook for 30 minutes.

2 Remove the potatoes and cook the grated sweet potatoes. Finish off by cooking the grated pumpkin.

3 Layer the vegetables in a bread pan and top with chives and lemon juice. Cover with cling wrap. Use a weight to press the terrine down. Refrigerate for 12 hours.

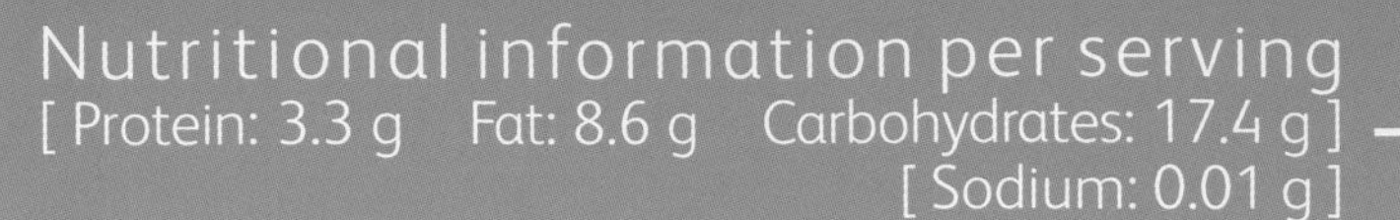

Nutritional information per serving
[Protein: 3.3 g Fat: 8.6 g Carbohydrates: 17.4 g]
[Sodium: 0.01 g]

Nutritious

This recipe, reminiscent of the sun, is a goldmine of vitamins, particularly vitamin C for vitality, and antioxidants such as lycopene and fibre. In addition, the olive oil contains monounsaturated fatty acids, which contribute to cardiovascular function.

Ratatouille

Serves **6** • Preparation **25** min • Cooking **31** min

- 1 onion, finely chopped
- 3 large tomatoes, diced
- 2 eggplant, cut into ¾ inch (2 cm) cubes
- 2 zucchinis, cut into ¾ inch (2 cm) cubes
- 2 green peppers, cut into ¾ inch (2 cm) cubes
- 2 red peppers, cut into ¾ inch (2 cm) cubes
- 5 cloves garlic, finely chopped
- 4 [spoon] olive oil
- Salt and fresh thyme

1 Put the oil in the ActiFry and heat for 1 minute. Cook the onion and peppers for 5 minutes.

2 Add the eggplant, zucchinis and garlic. Continue cooking for 15 minutes.

3 Finish off by adding the tomatoes for 10 minutes. Season the ratatouille and add a little fresh thyme.

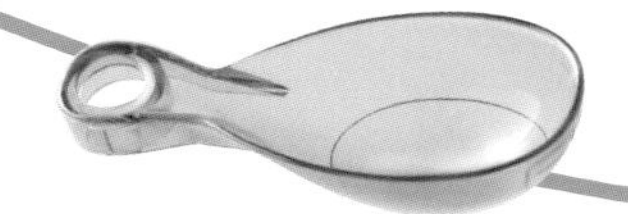

— 147 Cal

77 Cal

Nutritional information per serving
[Protein: 1.4 g Fat: 0.4 g Carbohydrates: 18.7 g]
[Sodium: 0 g]

Nutritious

Nectarines are very refreshing, thanks to their water content. In addition, they are a good source of vitamin C for vitality and a strong immune system, and they are rich in provitamin A, which protects the skin.

Lavender Nectarines

Serves **6** • Preparation **15** min • Cooking **7** min

- **6** nectarines, not too ripe
- **3** spoons liquid caramel or caramel sauce
- **6** sprigs lavender, stems removed

1 Dip the nectarines into boiling water for 30 seconds and cool immediately in cold water. Peel and cut into wedges.

2 Pour the caramel into the ActiFry and heat for 4 minutes. Add the nectarine wedges and cook for another 3 minutes.

3 Sprinkle with lavender when cooked.

Tip: Serve warm with vanilla or almond ice cream.

Nutritional information per serving
[Protein: 2.1 g Fat: 8 g Carbohydrates: 15.6 g]
[Sodium: 0 g]

Nutritious

This delicious dessert has few calories and tastes great!

Apricots with Almonds

Serves **6** • Preparation **5** min • Cooking **5** min

12	plump apricots, not too ripe
¼ cup	(**50 mL**) whole or flaked almonds
1	lemon juice
3 tbsp	(**45 mL**) butter
4	granulated sugar
6 tbsp	(**90 mL**) water

1 Add the butter and sugar to the ActiFry pan and pour in the water. Heat until syrupy. Add the lemon juice.

2 When the mixture boils, add the apricots, cut side down. Cook for 2 to 3 minutes, then turn over and cook for another 1 to 2 minutes, adding the almonds.

Tip: For a real treat, add a drop of apricot brandy at the end.

— 135 Cal

249 Cal

Nutritious

This delicious crumble is a treat that covers your fibre needs, which helps digestion, and contains complex carbohydrates to feel full, along with betacarotene, which has antioxidant properties.

Nutritional information per serving
[Protein: 26 g Fat: 9.3 g Carbohydrates: 6 g]
[Sodium: 0 g]

Apple-Mango Crumble

Serves **6** • Preparation **15** min • Cooking **15** + **20** min

- **5** apples, peeled and cut into cubes
- **1** ripe mango, cut into cubes
- ½ (spoon) honey
- ¼ (spoon) finely chopped fresh gingerroot
- ½ (spoon) finely chopped fresh mint leaves
- **1** (spoon) ground hazelnuts (optional)
- Unsweetened berry sauce (frozen)

For the crumble:

- **⅔ cup** (**150 mL**) all-purpose flour
- **¼ cup** (**50 mL**) butter, at room temperature
- **5** (spoon) granulated sugar

1. Put the apples and the honey in the ActiFry and cook for 15 minutes.
2. Add the mango, ginger and mint and cook for 5 minutes.
3. Serve in a glass: put the berry sauce on the bottom. Top with the fruit and sprinkle with a little crumble.

For the crumble:

1. Mix the flour and sugar in a bowl. Add the butter and mix with your fingertips (the dough should remain crumbly).
2. Put the preparation in the ActiFry and cook for 15 minutes, until the crumble is golden brown. Set aside in a bowl.

Tip: If the mango is not entirely ripe, start cooking it at the same time as the apples.

Nutritional information per serving
[Protein: 1.3 g Fat: 4.3 g Carbohydrates: 42.7 g]
[Sodium: 0 g]

Nutritious

This dessert helps you meet the day's vitamin and mineral needs.

ActiFried Apples and Bananas with Lime and Coriander

Serves **6** • Preparation **20** min • Cooking **15** min

6	apples, peeled and cut into ¾ inch (2 cm) cubes
4	bananas, peeled and cut into ¾ inch (2 cm) slices
2 tbsp	**(30 mL)** butter
	Zest of 4 limes, sliced
2	finely chopped coriander (cilantro)
2	sugar

1 Mix the apples and sugar in a bowl. Met the butter in the ActiFry and add the apple and sugar mixture. Cook for 10 minutes.

2 Add the bananas and cook for another 5 minutes.

3 Add the lime zests and the coriander just before serving.

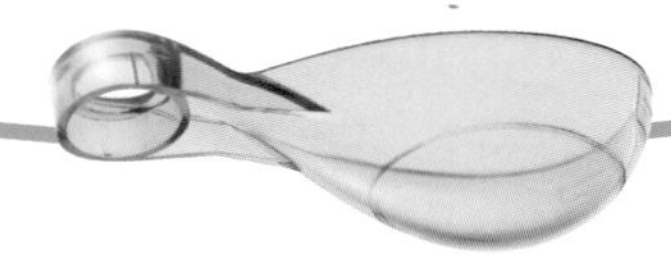

197 Cal

289 Cal

Nutritional information per serving
[Protein: 2.8 g Fat: 12 g Carbohydrates: 48 g]
[Sodium: 0 g]

Nutritious

This dessert, which mixes fresh fruit, dried fruit and nuts, contains vitamins, minerals and fibre, along with essential fatty acids that contribute to a healthy cardiovascular system.

Apple and Pear Wedges with Walnuts

Serves **6** • Preparation **15** min • Cooking **20** min

- **3** Granny Smith apples, peeled and cut into wedges
- **3** pears, peeled and cut into wedges
- **1 cup** (**250 mL**) walnuts
- **2** [spoons] walnut oil
- **2** [spoons] apple juice
- **1** [spoon] ground cinnamon
- **⅓ cup** (**75 mL**) raisins

1. Marinate the fruit in the oil and ground cinnamon for 30 minutes.
2. Put the fruit and the marinade in the ActiFry for 10 minutes. Add the apple juice, walnuts and raisins and cook for 10 more minutes.

Nutritional information per serving
[Protein: 2 g Fat: 4.7 g Carbohydrates: 33.5 g]
[Sodium: 0 g]

Nutritious

This very refreshing dessert contains good quantities of vitamins, especially A and C, along with fibre.

Peach, Mint and Grenadine Soup

Serves **6** • Preparation **25** min • Cooking **20** min

- **12** white peaches
- **1 tsp** (**5 mL**) orange-flower water
- **½ cup** (**125 mL**) grenadine
- **2** olive oil
- **1** Ras el hanout spice mix or ground cumin
- A few fresh mint leaves

1 Dip the peaches into boiling water for 20 seconds and then immediately into ice water. Peel and cut into wedges.

2 Put the orange-flower water, grenadine, oil and chosen spice into the ActiFry.

3 Add the peach wedges and cook for a few minutes.

Tip: Serve well chilled, with a few mint leaves and a scoop of sorbet.

— 173 Cal

174 Cal

Nutritional information per serving
[Protein: 1 g Fat: 0.4 g Carbohydrates: 46.3 g]
[Sodium: 0 g]

Nutritious

The pineapple and mango in this dessert contain fibre for good digestion, along vitamins such as vitamin C for vitality and A for healthy skin. Pineapple is an interesting source of vitamin C because this vitamin, which is fragile and oxidizes in contact with light, is protected by the fruit's thick skin until it is cut open.

Roast Pineapple and Mango

Serves **6** • Preparation **15** min • Cooking **20** min

- 1 pineapple
- 2 mangos, peeled
- Juice of 2 lemons
- 4 [spoons] honey
- pinch ground cinnamon

1 Cut off the top and bottom of the pineapple. Remove the skin, cut the fruit into 8 pieces lengthwise, remove the core and cut the flesh into ½ inch (1 cm) cubes. Cut the mangos the same size as the pineapple.

2 Put the mango pieces into the ActiFry and pour in 2 spoonfuls of honey. Cook for 10 minutes.

3 Add the pineapple and the remaining honey, lemon juice and cinnamon. Cook for an additional 10 minutes.

Tip: Serve warm with a scoop of vanilla ice cream.

Cooking

Potatoes

	TYPE	QUANTITY	ADD	COOKING TIME
Standard-sized fries 10 mm x 10 mm	Fresh	3 ⅓ lb (1.5 kg)	1 s. oil	45 min
		2 ¼ lb (1 kg)	¾ s. oil	38 min
		1 lb 11 oz (750 g)	½ s. oil	32 min
		1 lb 2 oz (500 g)	¼ s. oil	26 min
		9 oz (250 g)	⅛ s. oil	22 min
Traditional frozen fries	Frozen	2 ⅔ lb (1.2 kg)	none	40 min
		1 lb 11 oz (750 g)	none	27 min

s. = ActiFry spoonful

Meat and Poultry

	TYPE	QUANTITY	ADD	COOKING TIME
Chicken nuggets	Fresh	2 ⅔ lb (1.2 kg)	None	20 min
	Frozen	2 ⅔ lb (1.2 kg)	None	20 min
Chicken drumsticks	Fresh	9	None	30 min
Chicken legs	Fresh	3	None	35 min
Boneless chicken breast	Fresh	9 (about 2 ⅔ lb / 1.2 kg)	None	25 min
Spring rolls	Fresh	12 small	1 s. oil	12 min
Veal rolls	Fresh	9	1 s. oil	25 min
Lamb chops	Fresh	8	1 s. oil	20 min
Pork chops	Fresh	6	1 s. oil	20 min
Pork tenderloin	Fresh	9	1 s. oil	15 min
Rabbit back	Fresh	9	1 s. oil	20 min
Minced meat	Fresh	2 lb (900 g)	1 s. oil	15 min
	Frozen	1 ⅓ lb (600 g)	1 s. oil	15 min
Meatballs	Frozen	2 ⅔ lb (1.2 kg)	1 s. oil	20 min

times

Fish and Shellfish

	TYPE	QUANTITY	ADD	COOKING TIME
Breaded squid	Frozen	1 lb 2 oz (500 g)	None	14 min
Prawns	Cooked	1 ⅓ lb (600 g)	None	8 min
King prawns	Frozen	1 lb (450 g)	None	10 min

Vegetables

	TYPE	QUANTITY	ADD	COOKING TIME
Zucchinis	Fresh slices	2 ⅔ lb (1.2 kg)	1 s. oil + 5 fl oz (150 mL) water	30 min
Peppers	Fresh slices	2 ¼ lb (1 kg)	1 s. oil + 9 fl oz (250 mL) water	25 min
Mushrooms	Fresh quarters	2 ¼ lb (1 kg)	1 s. oil	20 min
Tomatoes	Fresh quarters	2 ¼ lb (1 kg)	1 s. oil	20 min
Onions	Fresh slices	1 lb 11 oz (750 g)	1 s. oil	30 min

Frozen Dishes

	TYPE	QUANTITY	ADD	COOKING TIME
Ratatouille	Frozen	2 ¼ lb (1 kg)	None	32 min
Fish and noodle stir-fry	Frozen	2 ¼ lb (1 kg)	None	22 min
Country fry	Frozen	2 ¼ lb (1 kg)	None	30 min
Savoy fry	Frozen	2 ¼ lb (1 kg)	None	25 min
Carbonara pasta	Frozen	2 ¼ lb (1 kg)	None	20 min
Paëlla	Frozen	2 ¼ lb (1 kg)	None	20 min
Fried rice	Frozen	2 ¼ lb (1 kg)	None	20 min
Chilli con Carne	Frozen	2 ¼ lb (1 kg)	None	15 min

Desserts

	TYPE	QUANTITY	ADD	COOKING TIME
Bananas	Slices	1 lb 9 oz (700 g) (7 bananas)	1 s. oil + 1 s. brown sugar	6 min
	Foil wrapped	3 bananas	None	20 min
Cherries	Whole	3 ⅓ lb (1.5 kg)	1 s. oil + 2 s. sugar	15 min
Strawberries	Cut in four	3 ⅓ lb (1.5 kg)	2 s. sugar	7 min
Apples	Cut in two	5	1 s. oil + 2 s. sugar	12 min
Pears	Pieces	3 ⅓ lb (1.5 kg)	2 s. sugar	12 min
Pineapple	Pieces	2	2 s. sugar	17 min

Recipe Index

KIDS

TEENS

by Chapter

FAMILY

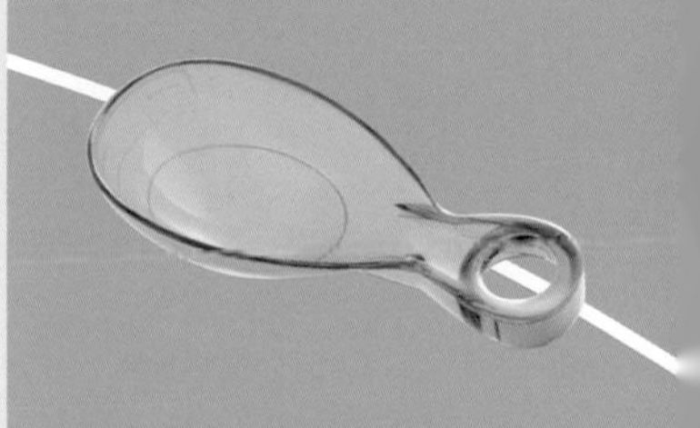

Ingredient

Eggs

Fish and seafood

Fruits

Apples

Apricots

Bananas

Mangoes

Nectarines

Peaches

Pears

Pineapple

Potatoes

Index

Rice

Semolina

Meat and poultry

Vegetables

My Recipes

My Recipes

NUTRITION
GOURMANDE™

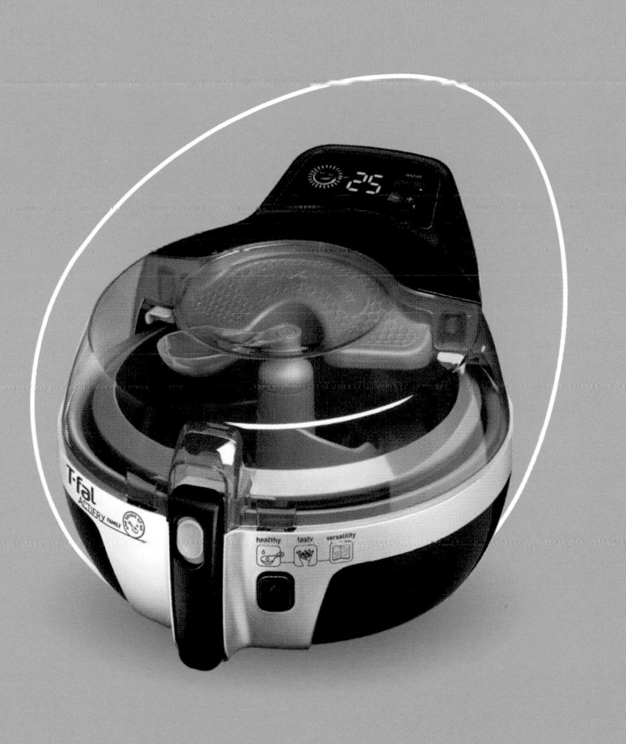
T·fal
healthy
tasty
versatility

Tous *en* cuisine !

T-fal®

Sommaire

T-fal : la Nutrition

Innover pour votre santé

La nutrition c'est, bien sûr, un régime varié et équilibré, mais ce n'est pas tout, car la nutrition c'est bien plus que les ingrédients. La façon de les cuisiner joue un rôle essentiel dans leur transformation nutritionnelle et organoleptique (goût, texture...).

Aussi parce que tous les appareils ne se valent pas, T-fal a développé une gamme dédiée à **la nutrition pour plus de plaisir** : des ustensiles ingénieux qui préservent l'intégrité nutritionnelle et exhalent le vrai goût des ingrédients.

Vous apporter des solutions uniques

T-fal investit dans la recherche pour créer des appareils au rendement nutrionnel unique, qui sont validées par des études scientifiques.

Vous informer

T-fal est depuis toujours le partenaire privilégié de votre alimentation en vous apportant rapidité, praticité et convivialité dans la préparation de vos repas.

Jour après jour, la gamme Nutrition Gourmande vous permet d'allier plaisir culinaire et régime équilibré en :

- favorisant et préservant les qualités des ingrédients essentiels à votre alimentation;
- limitant l'utilisation de matières grasses;
- favorisant le retour aux goûts et aux saveurs oubliés;
- limitant le temps passé à la préparation d'un repas.

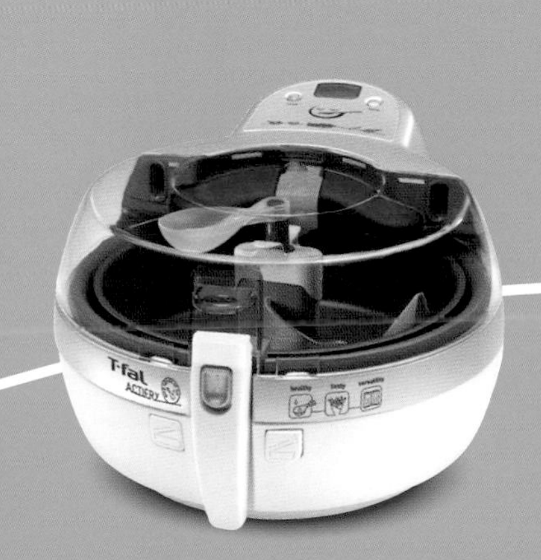

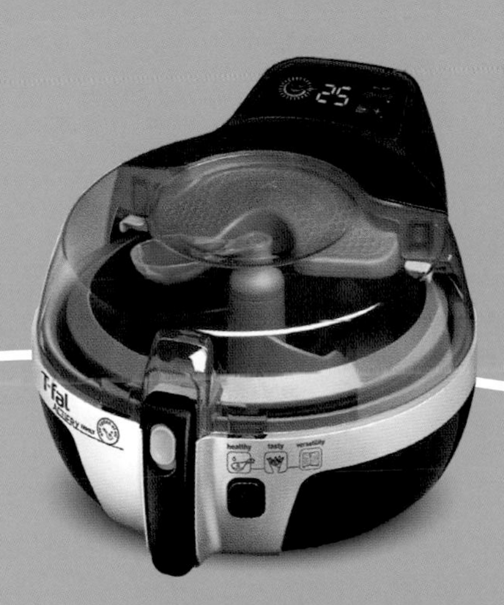

Gourmande

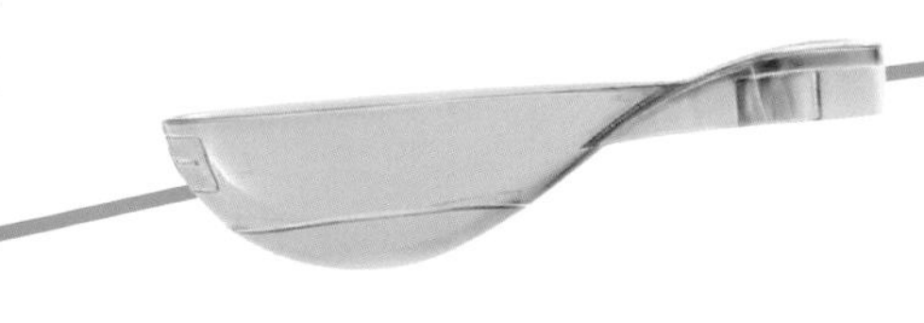

Il était une fois

ActiFry par T-fal

Depuis 150 ans, le Groupe SEB - Société d'Emboutissage de Bourgogne - crée son histoire sur l'innovation permanente et la conquête de nouveaux marchés. Faciliter la vie quotidienne des gens du monde entier, leur apporter des produits et des solutions nouvelles, leur procurant ainsi joie et bien-être, telle est sa vocation.

C'est ce mélange d'inventivité, d'ambition et de ténacité, comme notre attention auprès des consommateurs, qui a fait de notre Groupe le leader mondial des petits appareils ménagers.

Notre Société, implantée depuis son origine en Bourgogne, a su s'inspirer des valeurs historiques de cette célèbre région française; une gastronomie reconnue et un patrimoine culturel unique qui ont fortement influencé le mode de vie de ses habitants. Ce n'est donc pas un hasard si cette région a vu la naissance d'un procédé révolutionnaire de cuisson…

Aujourd'hui, au-delà de la simplicité dans votre vie quotidienne, nous sommes porteurs de vos instants gourmands et de bien d'autres expériences agréables, grâce à des produits parfaitement adaptés à une cuisine saine et savoureuse.

ActiFry la bourguignonne

Il y a bien longtemps que l'idée de faire des pommes de terre frites avec très peu d'huile avait germé… Ce sont notamment nos travaux de recherche avec des universités françaises sur le processus de cuisson qui nous ont permis d'aborder cette problématique sous un angle nouveau.

Cette connaissance nouvelle a permis d'établir précisément le rôle de l'huile dans la cuisson et les paramètres exacts de celle-ci pour obtenir à la fois le croustillant à l'extérieur et le moelleux à l'intérieur.

Une fois ce procédé connu et maîtrisé, il fallait le transposer dans un appareil domestique… Ce sont pas moins de cinq générations de prototypes et de mutiples tests organoleptiques qui ont été nécessaires pour parvenir à la qualité et au résultat souhaités.

Nos recherches et nos travaux de mise au point nous ont conduit aujourd'hui à déposer quatre brevets concernant ce procédé révolutionnaire.

Plus de 10 ans de recherche entre l'idée initiale et la première production "série" en janvier 2007. Résultat d'un travail d'équipe, ActiFry est aujourd'hui fabriquée à plusieurs milliers d'exemplaires par jour, en France, au cœur de la région Bourgogne!

ActiFry

ActiFry la révolutionnaire

ActiFry, c'est seulement une cuillerée d'huile pour 1,5 kg de vraies frites croustillantes à l'extérieur et moelleuses à l'intérieur, soit moins de 3% de matière grasse pour retrouver le goût des frites de nos grand-mères… En utilisant les bonnes huiles qui nous font du bien, ActiFry permet de varier les plats et les saveurs. Elle fait partie de notre gamme Nutrition Gourmande qui regroupe des technologies de pointe et tout le savoir-faire de T-fal au service du plaisir et de la santé.

ActiFry la Familiale

ActiFry a beaucoup voyagé et n'a pas fini de faire parler d'elle… Après avoir séduit plus de deux millions de consommateurs dans le monde entier, ActiFry a su s'adapter à leurs besoins et à leurs envies afin de satisfaire au mieux leurs papilles. Son talent de "cuisinière" est devenu incontestable et chaque consommateur se retrouvera dans ce livre de recettes saines et adaptées à tous âges et aux goûts de chacun : des recettes amusantes et gourmandes pour les enfants, des recettes faciles et savoureuses pour les ados, et des recettes pratiques et délicieuses pour la famille.

C'est aussi parce que la santé est primordiale pour chacun qu'ActiFry a séduit ces familles avisées du monde entier en alliant qualités nutritionnelles, bons goûts et praticité.

ActiFry la médiatique

Aujourd'hui, ce sont ses clients mais aussi les journalistes du monde entier qui viennent visiter son lieu de naissance, la ville française de Is-sur-Tille. Ils veulent comprendre quelle potion magique a pu permettre une telle innovation! Jusqu'aux paparazzis qui "mitraillent" sans relâche ActiFry lors de nos démonstrations et dégustations avec les familles du monde entier!

ActiFry l'ambitieuse

Et tout ceci n'est qu'un début, ActiFry n'attend que vous pour continuer d'alimenter son livre de recettes. Alors, si vos talents de cuisiniers peuvent accompagner le périple d'ActiFry, n'hésitez pas à visiter le site Nutrition Gourmande pour y ajouter vos recettes.

NUTRITION GOURMANDE™

www.nutritious-and-delicious.com

Les professionnels

ALLEMAGNE

Docteur JOHANNES M. PEIL, dirigeant de la Clinique du Sport Bad Nauheim et Président de l'Institut pour l'Alimentation Sportive

Les vitamines, les calories, les acides gras sont autant de facteurs importants pour évaluer la valeur nutritionnelle des aliments. Mais ils ne sont pas forcément en rapport avec le plaisir et avec nos critères de choix quotidiens en matière d'alimentation. Le goût, la rapidité et la facilité de préparation sont les points essentiels lorsque nous devons sélectionner les produits qui vont se retrouver sur nos tables.

ActiFry family permet d'associer rapidité, santé, saveur et praticité.

ActiFry family transforme chaque cuisine en un lieu de gourmet et de santé pour toute la famille. ActiFry family permet de respecter plus facilement la recommandation des médecins et des nutritionnistes qui nous demandent de consommer davantage d'aliments riches en nutriments, avec plus de vitamines et de minéraux par calorie. Et le plaisir est là. On n'est pas obligé de renoncer à ses mets favoris.

Le plaisir avec la santé et la saveur en supplément.

RUSSIE

Docteur MARIANA TRIFONOVA, Nutritionniste

Le concept d'alimentation saine pour un Russe moderne c'est la qualité de cuisson des aliments permettant d'en préserver la saveur et d'en réduire le temps. La gamme Nutrition Gourmande constitue la référence absolue en la matière. En ma qualité d'utilisateur spécialisé, je peux affirmer qu'elle répond à la fois aux exigences des diététiciens et à celles des Russes en matière d'électroménager permettant de cuisiner de délicieux aliments de haute qualité. Cette combinaison répond précisément aux postulats principaux de la doctrine diététique, qui n'est pas seulement une science de la nutrition, mais également un mode de vie à adopter.

en parlent

CANADA

Kim N. Arrey, RD, Diététiste et nutritionniste

Au Canada, de nos jours, les gens recherchent de nouvelles façons de manger sainement. La gamme Nutrition Gourmande de T-fal permet de préparer des aliments sains sans sacrifier les saveurs et, à la fois, de réduire le temps de cuisson. À titre de diététiste (et de maman qui travaille), je peux confirmer qu'ActiFry family fait tout à fait l'affaire! Les produits novateurs de la gamme Nutrition Gourmande répondent aux normes établies par des diététistes et aux demandes formulées par des Canadiens soucieux de leur santé. Vous pouvez préparer quelques-uns de vos plats préférés de toujours, mais en version plus saine, sans compromettre les saveurs tant appréciées ou encore, créer de nouvelles façons simples de préparer des repas savoureux à inclure dans votre répertoire.

FRANCE

Docteur CHRISTIAN RECCHIA, Docteur en médecine, Nutritionniste

Manger est avant tout un acte convivial et de partage, moment de plaisir toujours renouvelé, mais aussi instant précieux de bien-être et de santé. Bien se nourrir est un bon moyen pour mieux grandir et bien vieillir.

Les spécificités techniques d'ActiFry family permettent de consommer des frites et des pommes de terre à faible taux de matière grasse, ce qui est une aide précieuse pour lutter contre l'obésité et les maladies cardiovasculaires.

ActiFry family, c'est aussi la possibilité de cuire bien d'autres aliments : légumes, viandes, poissons, fruits.

Ce livre de recettes est un concentré haut en couleurs de plats savoureux et variés cuits dans un appareil révolutionnaire! Les assortiments ont été judicieusement choisis afin de vous donner un maximum de satisfaction à la fois d'un point de vue gustatif et d'un point de vue nutritionnel. Toutes les recettes ont été soigneusement élaborées en tenant compte des atouts nutritionnels de chaque ingrédient, et de leur intégration dans un menu équilibré.

Bien manger avec le guide

Nombre de portions du Guide alimentaire recommandé chaque jour

	Enfants			Adolescents		Adultes			
Âge (ans)	2-3	4-8	9-13	14-18		19-50		51+	
Sexe	Filles et garçons			Filles	Garçons	Femmes	Hommes	Femmes	Hommes
légumes et fruits	4	5	6	7	8	7-8	8-10	7	7
Produits céréaliers	3	4	6	6	7	6-7	8	6	7
Lait et substituts	2	2	3-2	3-4	3-4	2	2	3	3
Viandes et substituts	1	1	1-2	2	3	2	3	2	3

Le tableau ci-dessus indique le nombre de portions du Guide alimentaire dont vous avez besoin chaque jour dans chacun des quatre groupes alimentaires.

Le fait de consommer les quantités et les types d'aliments recommandés dans le Guide alimentaire canadien et de mettre en pratique les astuces fournies vous aidera à :

- Combler vos besoins en vitamines, minéraux et autres éléments nutritifs.
- Réduire le risque d'obésité, de diabète de type 2, de maladies du coeur, de certains types de cancer et d'ostéoporose.
- Atteindre un état de santé globale et de bien-être.

alimentaire Canadien

À quoi correspond une portion du Guide alimentaire ?
Regardez les exemples présentés ci-dessous.

Légumes frais, surgelés ou en conserve	Légumes feuillus	Fruits frais, surgelés ou en conserve	Jus 100 % purs
125 mL (1/2 tasse)	Cuits : 125 mL (1/2 tasse) Crus : 250 mL (1 tasse)	1 fruit ou 125 mL (1/2 tasse)	125 mL (1/2 tasse)

Pain	Bagel	Pains plats	Riz, boulgour ou quinoa, cuit	Céréales	Pâtes alimentaires ou couscous, cuits
1 slice (35 g)	1/2 bagel (45 g)	1/2 pita ou 1/2 tortilla (35 g)	125 mL (1/2 tasse)	Froides : 30 g Chaudes : 175 mL (3/4 tasse)	125 mL (1/2 tasse)

Lait ou lait en poudre (reconstitué)	Lait en conserve (évaporé)	Boisson de soya enrichie	Yogourt	Kéfir	Fromage
250 mL (1 tasse)	125 mL (1/2 tasse)	250 mL (1 tasse)	175 g (3/4 tasse)	175 g (3/4 tasse)	50 g (1 1/2 oz)

Poissons, fruits de mer, volailles et viandes maigres, cuits	Légumineuses cuites	Tofu	Oeufs	Beurre d'arachide ou de noix	Noix et graines écalées
75 g (2 1/2 oz)/125 mL (1/2 tasse)	175 mL (3/4 tasse)	150 g ou 175 mL (3/4 tasse)	2 oeufs	30 mL (2 c. à table)	60 mL (1/4 tasse)

Huiles et autres matières grasses

- Consommez une petite quantité, c'est-à-dire de 30 à 45 ml (2 à 3 c. à table) de lipides insaturés chaque jour. Cela inclut les huiles utilisées pour la cuisson, les vinaigrettes, la margarine et la mayonnaise.
- Utilisez des huiles végétales comme les huiles de canola, d'olive ou de soya.
- Choisissez des margarines molles faibles en lipides saturés et trans.
- Limitez votre consommation de beurre, margarine dure, saindoux et shortening.

Vrai ou

Testez vos connaissances sur les bénéfices santé des principaux nutriments que vous fournit votre alimentation.

Les protéines servent uniquement à nous donner de l'énergie.

Faux ! *Elles sont surtout indispensables au bon renouvellement des tissus et des cellules.*

Les lipides sont nécessaires pour le bon fonctionnement de nos cellules.

Vrai ! *Pas question de s'en priver ! Il faut 2 à 3 cuillerées de matières grasses variées, de préférence d'origine végétale, par jour pour assurer les apports nécessaires.*

Les glucides sont des sucres à éliminer totalement pour garder la ligne.

Faux ! *Pain, pâtes, riz, céréales fournissent des glucides à assimilation lente qui procurent une énergie durable et nécessaire, mais aussi une bonne satiété anti-grignotage.*

Les fibres, ça fait grossir!

Faux ! *Au contraire, les fibres du chou-fleur, du concombre, des épinards, des fruits rouges et des céréales régulent la digestion et diminuent l'absorption du cholestérol et la vitesse d'absorption des glucides.*

Le calcium est indispensable à tout âge.

Vrai ! *Tout au long de la vie, fromages, yogourts, petits suisses, fromages blancs doivent apporter au quotidien la dose de calcium suffisante pour maintenir une bonne ossature, aider à la contraction musculaire et prévenir l'ostéoporose.*

On trouve aussi bien du fer dans la viande et les abats que dans les huîtres, les œufs, les légumes secs et les fruits secs.

Vrai ! *Un bon apport en fer est indispensable à la formation des globules rouges. Attention cependant, l'absorption du fer d'origine animale est meilleure.*

Faux ?

La vitamine A se trouve uniquement dans le beurre, la crème et les jaunes d'œufs.

Faux !

On la trouve aussi dans les carottes, les épinards, le cresson, les abricots et la mangue sous forme de bêta-carotène. Anti-oxydante, elle favorise la croissance, agit sur la vue, la peau et la cicatrisation.

La vitamine C résiste très bien à une température de cuisson élevée.

Faux !

Fragile, elle nécessite une cuisson à la vapeur douce. On la trouve dans les légumes et les fruits. Anti-oxydante, elle agit sur la régénération cellulaire, favorise l'absorption du fer et renforce les défenses immunitaires.

Sans la vitamine D, le calcium ne peut pas renforcer les os.

Vrai !

L'organisme en synthétise la majeure partie sous l'effet du soleil. On trouve le reste dans le foie de poisson, les poissons gras, les abats, le jaune d'œuf, le lait entier et le fromage.

La vitamine E fait partie des anti-oxydants anti-vieillissement.

Vrai !

Présente dans l'huile, les fruits secs et oléagineux, elle protège les membranes des cellules et améliore la circulation sanguine.

Les vitamines du groupe B sont multi-fonctions et omniprésentes.

Vrai !

Présentes dans les légumes verts, les légumes secs, les carottes, le poisson, la viande, le jaune d'œuf et les céréales complètes, elles agissent sur l'état de la peau et des cheveux, mais aussi sur les systèmes nerveux et musculaire, les tissus et les organes et enfin sur la formation des globules rouges.

Pour bénéficier d'une multitude d'éléments nutritifs, variez au maximum votre alimentation.

Pourquoi faut-il vraiment varier le choix des huiles ?

Varier les huiles, c'est varier les saveurs en même temps que les apports. La gourmandise et la santé y trouvent toutes deux leur compte. Pourquoi s'en priver ?

Les corps gras alimentaires sont constitués de 3 catégories d'acides gras : *saturés* (AGS) qui augmentent le mauvais cholestérol, au contraire des *mono-insaturés* (AGMI) et *poly-insaturés* (AGPI) qui contribuent au bon fonctionnement du système cardio-vasculaire.

Limitez, d'une manière générale, les acides gras saturés : en excès, ils font monter le taux de mauvais cholestérol, le LDL, qui se dépose sur les parois de nos artères.

On les trouve dans les matières grasses qui figent à température ambiante, signe d'une forte teneur en acides gras saturés : les matières grasses d'origine animale (beurre, crème) et quelques huiles végétales (noix de coco, de palme, beurre de karité).

Choisissez de préférence des huiles végétales, riches en acides gras insaturés et poly-insaturés. Leur composition est variable. **L'idéal est donc de varier les huiles pour varier les apports (cf tableau) et les bénéfices :** huiles d'olive, de tournesol, de colza, de noix, de noisette, de pépin de raisin... Le choix est vaste et savoureux!

Les mono-insaturés AGMI

Ce sont les huiles *mono-insaturées* dites oléiques parce que leur teneur en acide oléique est supérieure à 50 % : olive, tournesol, noisette, colza, amande, pistache, noix de pécan... Les acides gras mono-insaturés forment la gaine de myéline autour des nerfs, régulent le métabolisme des lipides et font baisser le taux de cholestérol LDL. Notre organisme en produit par lui-même à partir du glucose.

Les poly-insaturés AGPI

Ces huiles contiennent deux types d'*acides gras poly-insaturés* : l'acide linoléique, précuseur des Oméga 6 et l'acide alpha-linolénique, précurseur des Oméga 3. Ce sont des acides gras à longues chaînes, aux vertus protectrices désormais reconnues, que le corps humain est incapable de fabriquer tout seul. Il doit impérativement les trouver dans l'alimentation quotidienne, d'où leur nom d'acides gras *essentiels*.

Bénéfices des

Oméga 6

L'acide linolénique favorise la baisse de la cholestérolémie totale avec diminution du LDL et du HDL cholestérol. Il contribue également à la formation de certaines hormones. On le trouve dans les huiles de tournesol, de maïs et de pépin de raisin.

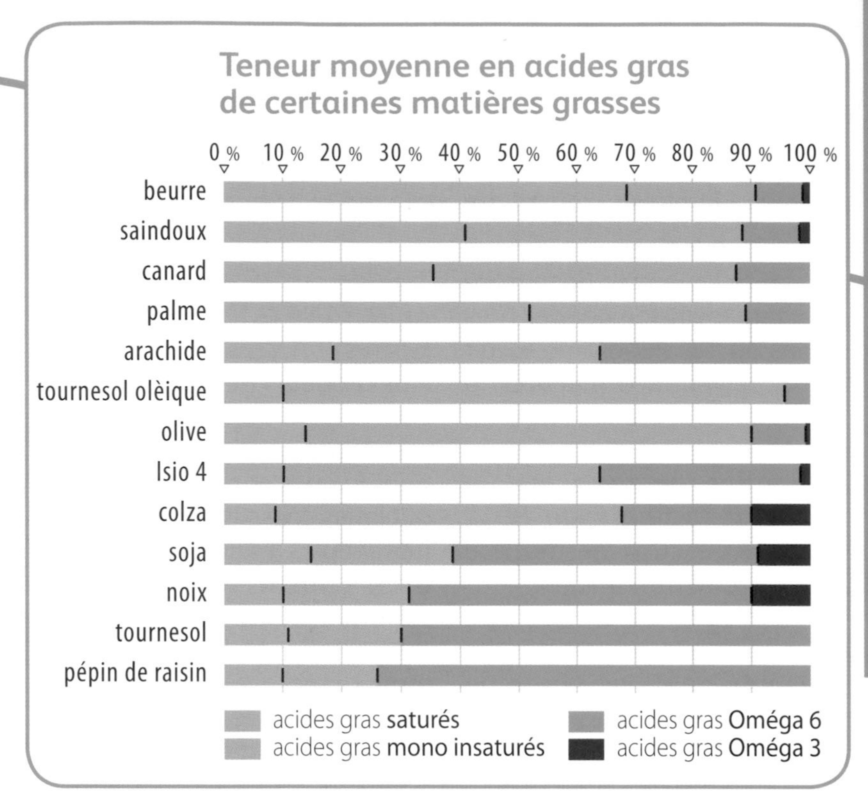

Bénéfices des

Oméga 3

L'acide alpha-linoléique réduit les triglycérides sanguins et permet la synthèse de dérivés qui contribuent à la fluidité du sang, avec un effet protecteur contre les maladies cardio-vasculaires. On le trouve dans les huiles de lin, de soja, de noix et de lupin. À noter : l'huile de colza est une huile à la fois oléique et linolénique.

Bien choisir ses matières grasses!

Gérez à la fois la quantité et la qualité des apports.

Limitez la quantité totale de graisses et de cholestérol : un minimum de matières grasses animales, des huiles végétales variées.

Réduisez fortement la quantité d'acides gras saturés.

Assurez-vous d'équilibrer les divers acides gras en privilégiant les huiles qui contiennent des acides gras insaturés et en particulier des poly-insaturés.

Variez les huiles pour obtenir un apport encore plus varié et complet en acides gras Oméga 3 et Oméga 6.

Petite histoire de la frite et de la pomme de terre

C'est la pomme de terre qui fait la frite! Un petit goût de fête qui met tout le monde d'accord sur le menu. Un plaisir croustillant, partagé avec bonheur partout dans le monde.

Quand l'explorateur Parmentier a rapporté la pomme de terre de son lointain voyage par-delà des océans au 18e siècle, il ne savait pas qu'il venait d'inventer la frite ! Depuis, le monde entier l'a adoptée...

La pomme de terre est un tubercule composé de 80% d'eau et de 20% de matière sèche, surtout de l'amidon.

Ce qu'il faut savoir : la frite plongée dans un bain d'huile bouillante perd une partie de son eau et absorbe les matières grasses à la place, d'où la mauvaise réputation de la frite.

La solution ActiFry family : grâce à son ingénieux système de remuage et de chauffage, **1 seule cuillerée d'huile suffit pour faire 1,5 kilo de frites** légères et dorées !

Plus d'odeurs de friture, plus de bain d'huile qui se dégrade. Un minimum de matières grasses dans la cuve et dans les frites. Et quelques conseils de préparation très simples à suivre.

Bien choisir sa pomme de terre : moins la pomme de terre est humide, plus elle est riche en matière sèche, plus elle croustille. La couleur dorée de la frite après cuisson dépend de sa teneur en sucre.

Les pommes de terre primeur sont souvent pauvres en sucre. Ensuite, tout au long du stockage, l'amidon se transforme en sucre ; les frites ont alors un goût plus sucré et une couleur plus brune (Agata, Monalisa).

Sa taille : en Europe, on apprécie les pommes de terre de taille petite et moyenne. Partout ailleurs, on les préfère très grosses.

La pomme de terre se conserve dans un endroit frais (6 à 8°C) à l'abri de la lumière.

Il y a plus de 400 variétés de pommes de terre en Europe. Plus de 4000 en Amérique du Sud où on la cultive depuis 8000 ans dans la Cordillère des Andes!

En France, Belgique et Hollande, on trouve la pomme de terre idéale pour les frites, la Bintje.

Mais aussi des variétés plus petites à chair ferme qui donnent de bons résultats : Charlotte, Franceline, mais aussi Chérie, Anabelle, Ratte, Nicola, Esmeralda, Pompadour...

Pour des frites plus moelleuses, choisir des variétés à teneur moyenne en matière sèche : Monalisa, Marabel, Vivi, Mélody.

Avec des pommes de terre à très faible taux de matières sèches, les frites seront molles : Agata, Spunta.

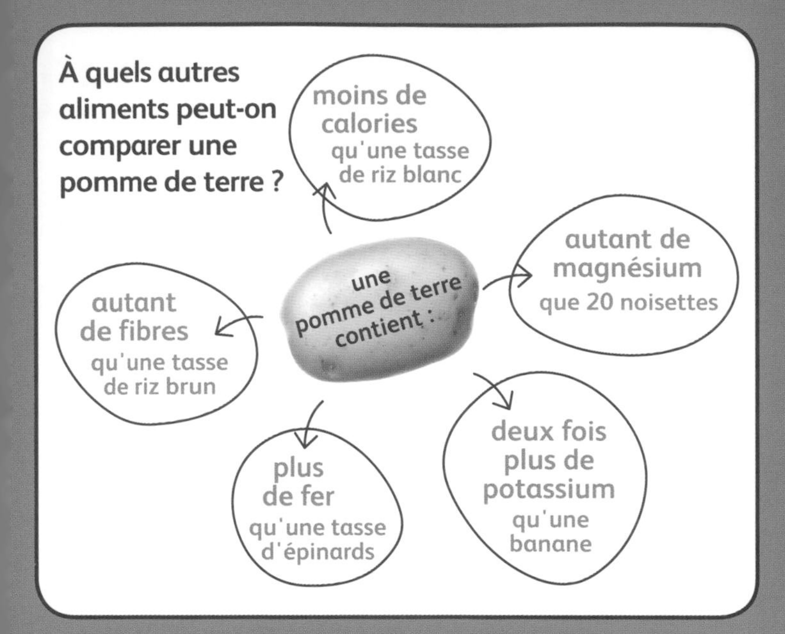

Vos frites avec ActiFry

Mieux vaut utiliser des pommes de terre idéales pour les frites.
Si vous avez choisi des pommes de terre nouvelles, ajoutez quelques minutes de cuisson supplémentaires au temps indiqué.
Si vous utilisez des frites surgelées, en général précuites, inutile de rajouter de l'huile.

Comment conserver vos pommes de terre pour faire des frites dans ActiFry ?

Les frites ne doivent pas coller entre elles. Comment l'éviter ? Une fois les pommes de terre pelées, lavez-les à grande eau avant de les couper en bâtonnets. Puis lavez-les à nouveau pour retirer un maximum d'amidon. Séchez vos frites avec soin dans un linge sec très absorbant. Assurez-vous que les bâtonnets sont bien secs avant de les mettre dans ActiFry.

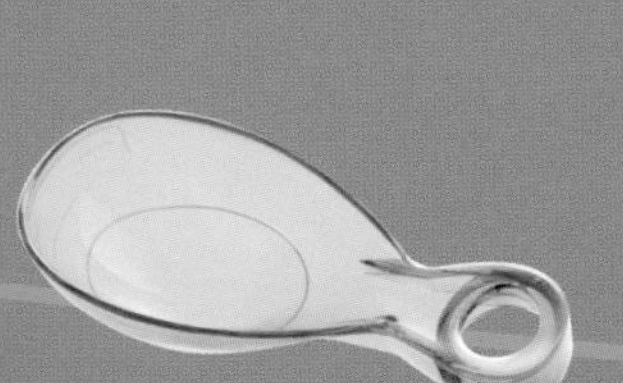

Où conserver la pomme de terre ?

Les meilleurs endroits pour conserver les pommes de terre sont : soit une bonne cave, soit un endroit frais (entre 6 et 8°C), à l'abri de la lumière.

Comment couper la pomme de terre ?

Très important! Selon la façon dont vous les coupez, vos frites seront plus ou moins croustillantes ou moelleuses. Plus elles sont fines, plus elles croustillent. Plus elles sont épaisses, plus elles sont moelleuses à l'intérieur. Variez la coupe en fonction de vos goûts :

- fines : 8 x 8 mm
- standard : 10 x 10 mm
- épaisses : 13 x 13 mm

Ne salez pas trop! Pensez à remplacer le sel par des épices ou des herbes…

La pomme de terre, c'est tout bon !

Si la frite dore avec un minimum de matières grasses, il n'y a aucune raison de s'en priver. Au contraire, c'est un petit plaisir à s'accorder qui permet de négocier avec soi-même ou avec les enfants une diminution des matières grasses et du sucre dans le reste de l'alimentation sans se sentir punis ou au régime.

L'important

Des menus équilibrés pour la semaine

Un régime équilibré n'est pas fondé sur un seul repas, mais plutôt sur les repas d'une semaine !

Il est donc primordial de varier ses menus

C'est pourquoi ce livre de recettes vous propose de nombreuses recettes originales réparties sur 2 semaines de menus équilibrés. Simples à mettre en œuvre, elles respectent grâce à ActiFry les qualités gustatives et nutritionnelles des aliments.

Le petit-déjeuner est un temps essentiel et privilégié de notre équilibre nutritionnel

Bien construit, ce premier repas de la journée permet non seulement à notre organisme de se réapprovisionner en énergie et en nutriments après une longue nuit de jeûne, mais il est également le garant d'une matinée efficace, sans grignotage et sans risque de "fringales".

Nous avons choisi de vous proposer un petit-déjeuner idéalement équilibré autour de **quatre piliers incontournables : une boisson, un produit laitier, un produit céréalier ainsi qu'un fruit,** entier, en jus ou en compote.

Où que vous portent vos préférences, veillez à ce que ces quatre fassent partie de votre petit déjeumer.

Il importe que vous sélectionniez vos produits avec soin pour leurs qualités nutritionnelles et gustatives, de sorte que ce petit-déjeuner utile soit le premier moment savoureux de votre journée !

Le dîner et le souper doivent fournir chacun ⅓ des apports de la journée

Ils se composent d'une entrée, d'un plat principal (viande ou poisson accompagné de féculents et de légumes verts), de fromage /d'un produit laitier et d'un fruit. Le secret est de varier votre alimentation sachant que tout est question de modération.

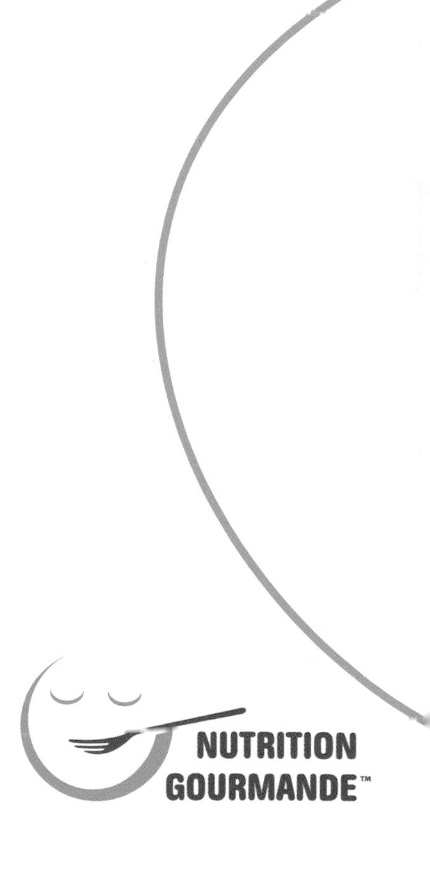

c'est l'équilibre

Nathalie
HUTTER LARDEAU
Nutritionniste

Bonne nouvelle! Vous n'êtes plus obligés de choisir entre l'équilibre et le plaisir de manger. C'est important quand on doit faire les menus pour satisfaire toute la famille. ActiFry family adapte sa contenance aux besoins et aux portions d'une famille de 6 personnes. Son plus grand intérêt reste de pouvoir cuisiner aussi bien les frites qu'une quantité de plats savoureux et faciles à faire avec un minimum de matières grasses. Un ustensile vraiment utile!

En tant que nutritionniste, je vois des parents se démener chaque jour pour manger moins gras, moins moins de sucre, surveiller le poids des enfants, le leur. Je les vois y arriver pendant un certain temps, puis renoncer. Ils craquent et reviennent à leurs vieilles habitudes alimentaires mauvaises pour la santé de toute la famille, à court et à long terme.

ActiFry family, c'est une chance de modifier en douceur votre façon de manger. Une chance de cuisiner moins gras sans même s'en rendre compte.

Dans ActiFry family, vous faites 1,5 kilo de vraies frites croustillantes avec seulement 1 cuillerée d'huile.

Pour atteindre tout naturellement l'équilibre sans vous forcer, il suffit de varier les plaisirs et les aliments au fil des menus que nous avons imaginés et calibrés avec soin pour toute la famille : viandes, poissons, légumes et fruits entrent dans la composition de toutes nos recettes.

Des recettes salées et sucrées avec un minimum de matières grasses, faciles à préparer, qui cuiront toutes seules dans ActiFry. Des recettes qui feront découvrir des goûts nouveaux aux plus petits. Des recettes assez exotiques ou originales pour séduire les ados .

De quoi refaire en douceur l'apprentissage de l'équilibre alimentaire pour toute la famille. Ettout cela, sans les priver de frites! Sans même avoir besoin d'en parler tant la transition se fera naturellement.

L'équilibre, ça doit être une histoire qui dure si l'on veut prévenir le surpoids et tous les problèmes de santé qui y sont liés.

Quand vous cuisinerez avec votre ActiFry family au jour le jour, dites-vous que vous cuisinez aussi pour l'avenir. C'est vital pour votre santé et celle de votre famille.

Exemples de menus

✚ Les recettes des plats indiqués en vert sont détaillées dans ce livre.

	Lundi *Journée Punch !*	Mardi *Au choix*	Mercredi *Déjeuner avec les enfants*
Petit-déjeuner	Chocolat chaud Baguette, beurre et miel Kiwi	Thé vert au jasmin Biscottes aux céréales et confiture Yogourt aromatisé Verre de jus d'orange	Café Bol de céréales et lait Compote
Dîner	Salade coleslaw ✚ Kebab ActiFrit (p111) Purée pommes de terre/ carottes Fromage cottage faible en gras Salade de fruits	Concombres à la crème ✚ Croquettes d'espadon au basilic (p48) Riz et brocoli Camembert Ananas en tranche	Jeunes pousses de laitue, tomates et noix Cuisse de poulet ✚ Frites (p28) Fromage cottage faible en gras + dés de banane
Souper	✚ Légumes à l'italienne (p132) Tagliatelles fraîches Jambon blanc Yogourt aux fruits	Poêlée de légumes forestiers et dés de bacon ✚ Halva à la semoule (p55)	✚ Tortillas d'œufs brouillés à la ActiFry (p83) Assiette de crudités (salade verte, carottes râpées, betteraves) Emmental Fruit de saison

équilibrés - SEMAINE 1

Jeudi *Journée pressée !*	Vendredi *Soirée entre copains*	Samedi *Au choix*	Dimanche *Repas familial*
Chicorée Fromage cottage et fruits secs	Capuccino Bol de céréales et lait Fromage cottage ½ pamplemousse	Thé au caramel Baguette et emmental Salade de petits fruits	Café viennois Croissant Yogourt à la vanille Smoothie maison
Taboulé ✣ Crevettes à la créole très piquantes (p79) Gratin de zucchinis et aubergines Fruit de saison	Salade chou rouge et vinaigrette à la moutarde à l'ancienne ✣ Pilons de volaille épicés (p72) Quinoa au cumin Yogourt nature Poire pochée	Salade de tomate, feta et basilic ✣ Shawarma au poulet (p43) Légumes sautés avec riz brun Pêches au sirop	✣ Moules marinières aux tomates-cerises et basilic (p120) Salade de mesclun et vinaigrette au vinaigre balsamique Clafoutis des vendanges (raisins blancs et noirs)
✣ Haricots rouges à la sauce tomate (p51) Viande de bœuf hâchée Salade de fruits rouges et crème anglaise	Une tranche de saumon fumé sur toast aux céréales et zeste de citron ✣ Haricots verts étuvés à la sauge fraîche et amandes (p131) Fromage en crème Quartiers de mangue	✣ Terrine de légumes râpés avec citron et ciboulette (p135) 1 œuf à la coque + mouillettes Yogourt et abricots	Bouchées vapeur à la crevette ✣ Riz cantonais (p84) Fromage en crème avec des litchis

Exemples de menus

Les recettes des plats indiqués en vert sont détaillées dans ce livre.

	Lundi *Journée Rééquilibre*	Mardi *Au choix*	Mercredi *Dîner entre amis*
Petit-déjeuner	Café au lait Pain complet, beurre et miel Compote	Infusion de menthe poivrée mélisse Bol de lait, céréales et dés de banane	Café Biscottes aux céréales, confiture Fromage en crème Verre de jus d'agrumes
Dîner	Carottes râpées au jus de citron Pavé de saumon à la moutarde à l'ancienne Purée de pois cassés Mozzarella de lait écrémé Abricots aux amandes (p140)	Avocat Lapin au piment d'Espelette (p104) Polenta et tomates cerise Yogourt nature Fruit de saison	Radis roses Escalope de veau à la crème légère Purée de potiron à la noix de muscade Pain complet Pommes et bananes Acti-Frites à la lime et coriandre (p144)
Souper	Tofu ActiFrit à l'espagnole (p128) Salade de roquette Roquefort Salade de fruits	Pamplemousse aux crevettes Sauté méditerranéen de légumes (p123) Tarte aux pommes Verre de lait	Œuf cocotte au saumon fumé Pommes de terre aux champignons (p35) Fromage cottage Compote pomme rhubarbe

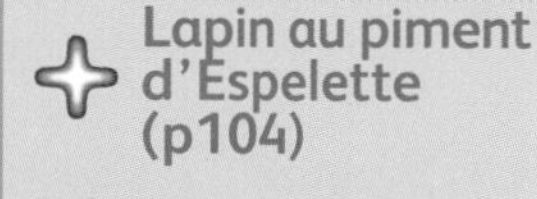

équilibrés - SEMAINE 2

Jeudi *Au choix*	Vendredi *Petit-déjeuner Énergie !*	Samedi *Soirée festive*	Dimanche *Journée Plaisir & Cuisine*
Capuccino Baguette, miel Verre de lait Kiwi	Thé à la vanille Bol de lait et céréales Compote	Thé à la cannelle Brioche Yogourt et coulis de fruits	Chocolat viennois Crêpes à la confiture Salade de fruits
Salade de chou blanc et pomme verte  **Porc en bâtonnets (p67)** Julienne de légumes de saison Fromage suisse Flan vanille	Betteraves rouges râpées 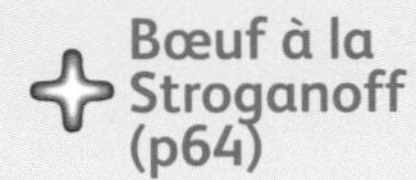 **Bœuf à la Stroganoff (p64)** Sauce chili Fromage cheddar	Assiette de crudités 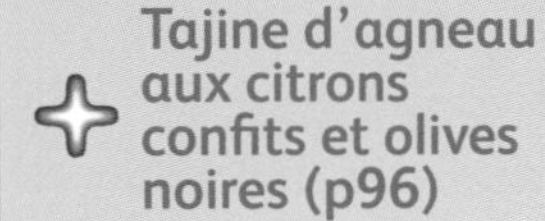 **Tajine d'agneau aux citrons confits et olives noires (p96)** Semoule semi complète Fromage cottage Fruit de saison	Salade verte **Petite friture de poissons à la sauce tartare (p47)** Zucchinis poêlées Panna Cotta aux fruits rouges
Risotto tomates confites et oignons verts (p124) Compote d'agrumes	**Sauce à la bolognaise (p100)** Pâtes fraîches Emmental râpé Fruit de saison	Croque-monsieur Salade de légumes de saison **Pommes à la cannelle (p56)**	Tzatziki, tarama et toasts de pain de mie aux céréales Tomates cerises, bâtonnets de carottes et sauce fromage blanc Jus de tomate **Nectarines à la lavande (p139)**

Temps de l'enfance

Moments de découvertes

Information nutritionnelle par portion
[Protéines : 5,2 g   Lipides : 2,5 g   Glucides : 41,5 g]
[Sodium : 0,02 g]

Nutrition

Les pommes de terre font partie du groupe des féculents qui vous fournissent des glucides complexes et vous évitent d'avoir faim entre les repas. Ils doivent donc être intégrés à chaque repas. La cuisson dans ActiFry vous permet de les cuisiner avec très peu de matière grasse et des huiles de bonne qualité.

Les vraies frites

Pour **6** personnes • Préparation **15** min • Cuisson **45** min

1,5 kg (3 lb) de pommes de terre épluchées et lavées

1 (cuillère) d'huile végétale

Sel

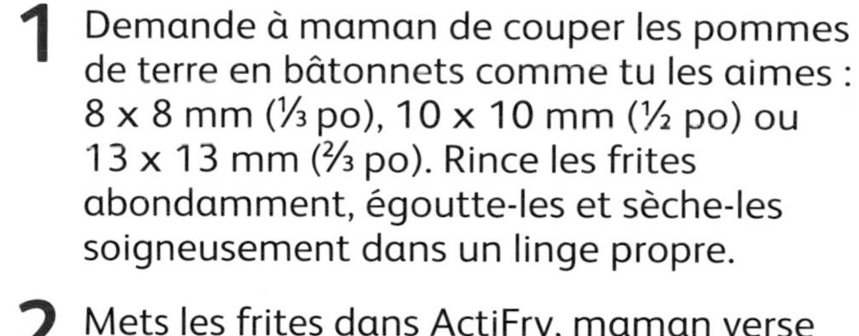

1 Demande à maman de couper les pommes de terre en bâtonnets comme tu les aimes : 8 x 8 mm (⅓ po), 10 x 10 mm (½ po) ou 13 x 13 mm (⅔ po). Rince les frites abondamment, égoutte-les et sèche-les soigneusement dans un linge propre.

2 Mets les frites dans ActiFry, maman verse l'huile sur les frites. C'est cuit en 45 min. Tu sales. C'est prêt.

Le temps de cuisson peut varier selon la variété de la pomme de terre et de l'épaisseur de la frite.

— **198** kcal

le sais-tu ?

La pomme de terre est le quatrième aliment le plus cultivé dans le monde après le riz, le blé et le maïs.

le sais-tu ?
L'amande est le fruit de l'amandier.
Une fois séchée, elle est utilisée de différentes façons :
entière, grillée, effilée, pilée,
en pâte, en crème, en lait
et même en sirop d'orgeat.
amandes
en poudre

Information nutritionnelle par portion
[Protéines : 6,7 g Lipides : 10,2 g Glucides : 42,8 g]
[Sodium : 0,02 g]

Nutrition

Oui, cette recette contient des féculents, mais elle contient également une bonne quantité d'acides gras essentiels, comme on en trouve dans l'huile de noisette et les amandes, qui contribuent au développement d'un système nerveux sain.

Frites aux amandes

Pour **6** personnes • Préparation **15** min • Cuisson **45** min

1,5 kg (3 lb) de pommes de terre épluchées et lavées
1 d'huile végétale
2 d'huile de noisette
3 d'amandes en poudre

1 Demande à maman de couper les pommes de terre en bâtonnets de 1 cm (½ po) d'épaisseur. Rince les bâtonnets abondamment, égoutte-les et sèche-les soigneusement dans un linge propre.

2 Mélange dans un bol les huiles et la poudre d'amandes.

3 Mets les bâtonnets dans ActiFry et maman verse le mélange uniformément sur les frites. 45 min. et c'est prêt !

Information nutritionnelle par portion
[Protéines : 9,3 g   Lipides : 21,7 g   Glucides : 53,8 g]
[Sodium : 0,9 g]

Nutrition

Modifiez cette recette en y ajoutant d'autres ingrédients comme des cacahuètes et des croustilles à saveur de bacon. Cette recette est plus gourmande que les autres recettes de frites cuisinées dans ActiFry c'est pourquoi elle doit être réservée à certaines occasions.

Frites cacahuètes et bacon

Pour **6** personnes • Préparation **20** min • Cuisson **55** min

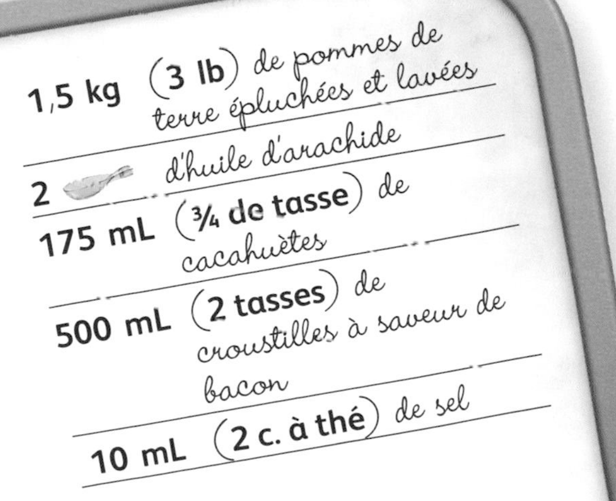

- **1,5 kg** (**3 lb**) de pommes de terre épluchées et lavées
- **2** [cuillère] d'huile d'arachide
- **175 mL** (**¾ de tasse**) de cacahuètes
- **500 mL** (**2 tasses**) de croustilles à saveur de bacon
- **10 mL** (**2 c. à thé**) de sel

1 Demande à maman de couper les pommes de terre en bâtonnets de 1 cm (½ po) d'épaisseur. Rince les bâtonnets abondamment, égoutte-les et sèche-les soigneusement dans un linge propre. Mets les bâtonnets dans ActiFry, maman rajoute l'huile et fait cuire pendant 45 min.

2 Demande à maman de réduire en poudre les croustilles avec le sel, dans un mélangeur. Pendant ce temps, concasse les cacahuètes. Ensuite mélange le tout.

3 Au bout de 45 min., maman ouvre ActiFry et répartit le mélange sur les frites. Encore 10 min. de cuisson et c'est prêt.

— 430 kcal

le sais-tu ?

L'arachide est une plante annuelle qui enterre ses fruits, les cacahuètes, après fécondation. Elle est originaire du Mexique.

le sais-tu ?

Le règne des champignons comprend 50 000 espèces, mais seulement quelques centaines sont comestibles.

Information nutritionnelle par portion
[Protéines : 5,9 g   Lipides : 9,2 g   Glucides : 32,8 g]
[Sodium : 0,03 g]

Nutrition

Cette recette fournit à votre régime des glucides complexes. Ceux-ci constituent un des principaux carburants de l'organisme et évitent les "petits creux" entre les repas.

Pommes de terre aux champignons

Pour **6** personnes • Préparation **5** min • Cuisson **47** min

- 1 kg (2 lb) de pommes de terre épluchées, lavées
- 250 g (8 oz) de champignons de Paris coupés en quartiers
- 1 oignon haché fin
- 175 mL (¾ de tasse) de crème de table à 18 %
- 1 [cuillère] d'huile végétale
- Sel et poivre

1. Demande à maman de couper les pommes de terre en cubes. Rince-les, égoutte-les et sèche-les dans un linge propre.
2. Maman fait chauffer l'huile dans ActiFry et met à cuire les oignons pendant 7 min. Lorsqu'ils commencent à devenir translucides, ajoute les cubes de pomme de terre. Laisse cuire 25 à 30 min. jusqu'à ce qu'ils soient presque cuits.
3. Ajoute ensuite les champignons et laisse encore cuire 7 min. Verse ensuite la crème fraîche et laisse cuire 2 à 3 min. Maman assaisonne.

Information nutritionnelle par portion
[Protéines : 4,8 g Lipides : 12,9 g Glucides : 36,7 g]
[Sodium : 0,02 g]

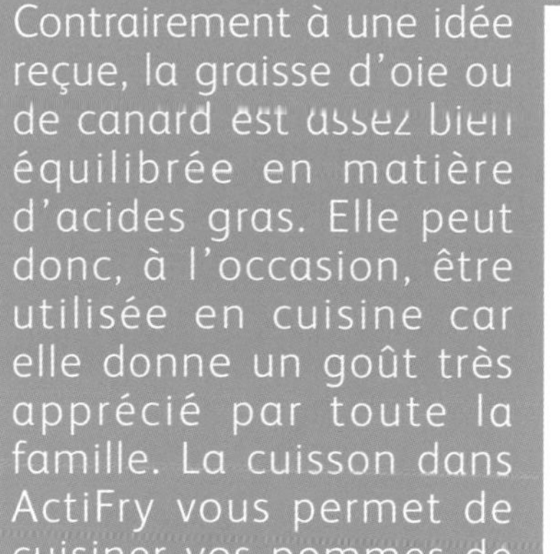

Nutrition

Contrairement à une idée reçue, la graisse d'oie ou de canard est assez bien équilibrée en matière d'acides gras. Elle peut donc, à l'occasion, être utilisée en cuisine car elle donne un goût très apprécié par toute la famille. La cuisson dans ActiFry vous permet de cuisiner vos pommes de terre avec très peu de matière grasse.

Pommes sarladaises

Pour **6** personnes • Préparation **20** min • Cuisson **47** min

- **1,25 kg** (2 ½ lb) de pommes de terre épluchées, lavées
- **5** [cuillère] de graisse d'oie ou de canard
- **5** gousses d'ail hachées
- **1** bouquet de persil haché
- Sel et poivre

1 Demande à maman de couper les pommes de terre en rondelles d'environ 3 mm (⅛ po) d'épaisseur. Rince les rondelles de pommes de terre, égoutte-les et essuie-les dans un linge propre.

2 Maman fait fondre la graisse pendant 2 min. dans ActiFry et tu ajoutes les rondelles de pommes de terre. Laisse cuire 35 min.

3 Ajoute ensuite l'ail dans la cuve et laisse cuire pendant 10 min. Saupoudre de persil et assaisonne.

— 272 kcal

le sais-tu ?

L'ail est une plante herbacée (c'est-à-dire qui a la forme d'une herbe) assez grande. Nous mangeons sa racine, formée de gousses et utilisée comme condiment.

278 kcal

Nutrition

Cette recette allie à la fois les bénéfices des pommes de terre nouvelles (vitamines, minéraux et glucides complexes), des crevettes (protéines de bonne qualité et peu de matière grasse) et les effets bénéfiques de l'ail sur la circulation sanguine. Les pommes de terre nouvelles sont plus riches que les autres en vitamine C et en minéraux comme le magnésium aux propriétés anti stress. Des qualités qui sont encore mieux préservées quand on ne les pèle pas. Cette recette permet aux enfants d'apprécier les crevettes grâce à la présence des pommes de terre.

le sais-tu ? La tomate n'est pas un légume, mais un fruit. On trouve plusieurs variétés : tomate ronde ou allongée, tomate cerise, en grappe ou côtelée, cœur de bœuf.

Information nutritionnelle par portion
[Protéines : 11,5 g Lipides : 7,8 g Glucides : 45,2 g]
[Sodium : 0,4 g]

Pommes de terre nouvelles, ail, tomates séchées et crevettes

Pour **6** personnes • Préparation **25** min • Cuisson **45** min

1 kg (**2 lb**) de pommes de terre nouvelles
20 gousses d'ail en chemises
3 [cuillères] d'huile d'olive
20 tomates séchées
20 crevettes crues décortiquées
125 mL (**½ tasse**) de persil haché
2 grosses pincées de fleur de sel

1 Lave les pommes de terre sans les éplucher et sèche-les soigneusement.

2 Demande à maman de verser l'huile dans ActiFry, mets les pommes de terre nouvelles et l'ail. Laisse cuire pendant 35 min.

3 Ajoute ensuite les crevettes, les tomates séchées, la fleur de sel et laisse cuire 10 min. Ajoute le persil au dernier moment.

Information nutritionnelle par portion
[Protéines : 36,3 g Lipides : 16,2 g Glucides : 29,5 g]
[Sodium : 0,3 g]

Escalopes viennoises

Pour **6** personnes • Préparation **20** min • Cuisson **15** min

- **750 g** (**1 ½ lb**) d'escalopes de veau coupée en petits morceaux de 30 g (1 oz)
- **3x1** d'huile de colza
- **300 mL** (**1 ¼ tasse**) de chapelure fine
- **100 g** (**⅔ de tasse**) de farine tout-usage
- **6** œufs battus
- **2** citrons en jus
- Sel et poivre

Nutrition

Alliance parfaite de protéines de bonne qualité (veau) pour la constitution des muscles, d'acides gras équilibrés (huile de pépins de raisin et veau) pour le bon fonctionnement cardio-vasculaire et de glucides complexes (farine, chapelure) pour la satiété, cette recette sera idéalement accompagnée d'épinards ou de salade.

1 Passe d'abord les escalopes dans la farine, puis dans dans les oeufs battus et en dernier dans la chapelure. Recommence les mêmes étapes une deuxième fois et demande à maman de mettre le tout au réfrigérateur pendant ½ heure.

2 Maman fait chauffer une cuillerée d'huile de colza dans ActiFry et met ⅓ de la viande à plat pour une cuisson de 10 à 15 min.

3 Continuer les tournées jusqu'à ce que toute la viande soit cuite.

Conseil : Pour la dorure, rajoutez un petit peu d'eau dans les jaunes d'œufs battus.

le sais-tu ?

La chapelure est constituée de pain séché et broyé.
En cuisine, elle sert à paner des aliments, à épaissir une sauce ou à saupoudrer un plat à gratiner.

166 kcal
le sais-tu ?
Le mot vinaigre vient de "vin aigre".
Le vinaigre est en fait du vin qu'on a laissé vieillir,
et qui tourne à l'aigre.
marinade

Information nutritionnelle par portion
[Protéines : 23,6 g Lipides : 4,9 g Glucides : 7,6 g]
[Sodium : 1,5 g]

Nutrition

Cette recette vous fournit des protéines de bonne qualité pour le fonctionnement musculaire tout en faisant découvrir de nouvelles saveurs à vos enfants.

Shawarma au poulet

Pour **6** personnes • Préparation **10** min • Cuisson **10-15** min

- **750 g** (1 ½ lb) de poitrines de poulet désossées et sans peau
- **1** c. de cumin en poudre
- **1** c. de Raz el hanout (ou épices Shawarma)
- **3** gousses d'ail finement hachées
- **2** oignons finement hachés
- **2** c. de vinaigre
- **2** c. d'huile végétale
- Sel et poivre

1 Demande à maman d'émincer le poulet.

2 Mélange tous les ingrédients et mets au réfrigérateur pendant 12 heures pour que le poulet soit bien mariné.

3 Mets le poulet mariné dans ActiFry et laisse cuire 10 à 15 min. Assaisonne à ton goût.

Information nutritionnelle par portion
[Protéines : 46,9 g Lipides : 18,7 g Glucides : 16,3 g]
[Sodium : 0,3 g]

Nutrition

La cuisson dans ActiFry permet de faire de savoureuses boulettes de viande cuites sans ajout de matière grasse. L'utilisation du fromage complète très bien les apports calciques de la journée. Ce dernier est tout particulièrement important pour la solidité osseuse et la croissance des enfants.

Boulettes de viande frites

Pour **6** personnes • Préparation **15** min • Cuisson **20** min

- **1 kg** (**2 lb**) de viande hachée (mélange de veau 60 % et de porc 40 %)
- **2** [cuillères] de cumin
- **150 g** (**5 oz**) de fromage Gruyère
- **3** tranches de mie de pain
- **150 mL** (**⅔ de tasse**) de lait écrémé
- **2** œufs
- **½** tasse de persil haché
- **150 mL** (**⅔ tasse**) de farine
- **1** [cuillère] d'huile de colza
- Sel et poivre

1 Demande à maman de mélanger dans un saladier la viande hachée, le cumin, le persil, les œufs, les tranches de mie de pain trempées dans le lait, le sel et le poivre.

2 Aide maman à confectionner des boulettes ayant chacune 4 cm (1½ po) de diamètre. Incorpore des morceaux de Gruyère au milieu de chaque boulette.
Il faut bien refermer la boulette de façon que le fromage ne coule pas pendant la cuisson.

3 Roule ensuite les boulettes dans la farine et mets-les à cuire pendant 20 min dans ActiFry, avec l'huile.

431 kcal
le sais-tu ?
Le pain est fait de farine, d'eau, de sel et de levure.
La mie est la partie molle du pain.
Comté
farine

426 kcal —

Nutrition

Le poisson est un aliment d'une haute valeur nutritionnelle, par la qualité de ses protéines, ses acides gras ainsi que sa teneur en iode. Cette recette vous aidera à le faire apprécier à vos enfants.

le sais-tu ?

Il existe 3 sortes de poivres :

- le poivre vert, des baies récoltées alors qu'elles ne sont pas encore mûres.
- le poivre blanc, des baies mûres dont on a enlevé l'écorce.
- le poivre noir, des baies mûres avec leur écorce, fermentées puis séchées.

Information nutritionnelle par portion
[Protéines : 33,5 g Lipides : 22,3 g Glucides : 21,3 g]
[Sodium : 0,3 g]

Petite friture de poissons
à la sauce tartare

Pour **6** personnes • Préparation **15** min
• Cuisson **10-15** min
selon la taille des poissons

Friture :

- **1 kg** (**2 lb**) de poissons à friture (ablettes, goujons, petit éperlans...)
- **250 mL** (**1 tasse**) de farine tout-usage
- **4** d'huile végétale
- Sel, poivre

Sauce tartare :

- **250 mL** (**1 tasse**) de crème sure
- **6** cornichons finement hachés
- **4** de câpres finement hachés
- **2** citrons en jus
- **2** échalotes finement hachées
- **2** de persil plat haché
- Sel et poivre

1 Prépare la sauce tartare : mélange tous les ingrédients et assaisonne.

2 Demande à maman de rincer, sécher, fariner et assaisonner les petits poissons. Mets les poissons dans ActiFry, verse l'huile et laisse cuire pendant 10 à 15 min. jusqu'à ce qu'ils soient dorés et croustillants.

3 Maman les retire et les égoutte sur du papier absorbant. À déguster avec la sauce tartare.

Information nutritionnelle par portion
[Protéines : 26,9 g Lipides : 13,8 g Glucides : 24,8 g]
[Sodium : 0,2 g]

Croquettes d'espadon au basilic

Nutrition

Un plat extrêmement savoureux, qui combine les protéines du poisson avec celles des œufs. Grâce au mélange des diverses saveurs, ce plat peut plaire aux personnes qui n'apprécient pas les plats à base de produits de la mer en tant que tel ou faire découvrir le goût du poisson aux enfants.

Pour **6** personnes • Préparation **15** min • Cuisson **12** min

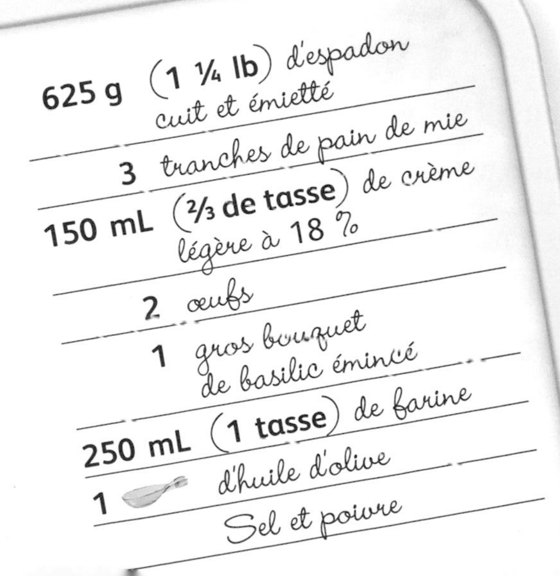

- **625 g** (**1 ¼ lb**) d'espadon cuit et émietté
- **3** tranches de pain de mie
- **150 mL** (**⅔ de tasse**) de crème légère à 18 %
- **2** œufs
- **1** gros bouquet de basilic émincé
- **250 mL** (**1 tasse**) de farine
- **1** [cuillère] d'huile d'olive
- Sel et poivre

1 Demande à maman de mélanger l'espadon, la moitié de l'huile, la mie ramollie au préalable dans la crème, les œufs et l'assaisonnement.

2 Rajoute le basilic et forme des croquettes d'environ 30 g (1 oz) chacune à l'aide d'une poche à pâtisserie en plastique.

3 Farine chaque croquette et maman les met à cuire dans ActiFry dans l'huile chaude pendant 12 min. environ.

Conseil : Fais des petites croquettes bien compactes et n'en cuis pas trop à la fois.

339 kcal
48 | 49
TEMPS DE L'ENFANCE
le sais-tu ?
La crème est la matière grasse du lait.
À l'origine, la crème fraîche était une spécialité française.
farine

le sais-tu ?

Le haricot est le fruit d'une plante d'Amérique centrale et du Sud.
Le mot " haricot " désigne à la fois le fruit, la graine et la plante.

Information nutritionnelle par portion
[Protéines : 7,7 g Lipides : 4,5 g Glucides : 27,7 g]
[Sodium : 0,4 g]

Nutrition

Les légumes secs comme les haricots rouges sont une source très intéressante de protéines végétales qui, même si elles sont moins complètes en acides aminés que les protéines animales, sont indispensables à notre alimentation. Ce plat sera idéal au souper pour les enfants.

Haricots rouges à la sauce tomate

Pour **6** personnes • Préparation **15** min • Cuisson **25** min

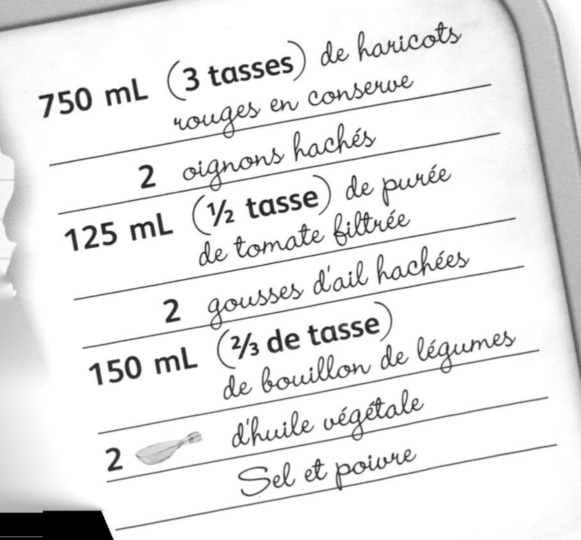

- **750 mL (3 tasses)** de haricots rouges en conserve
- **2** oignons hachés
- **125 mL (½ tasse)** de purée de tomate filtrée
- **2** gousses d'ail hachées
- **150 mL (⅔ de tasse)** de bouillon de légumes
- **2** [cuillères] d'huile végétale
- Sel et poivre

1. Demande à maman de faire chauffer l'huile et de mettre à cuire les oignons et l'ail pendant 5 min.
2. Ajoute les haricots rouges égouttés, la purée de tomates et le bouillon.
3. Maman assaisonne et laisse cuire 20 min.

Option : Si tu ajoutes de la viande hachée au début de la cuisson, tu obtiendras un chili.

Information nutritionnelle par portion
[Protéines : 8,1 g Lipides : 9,3 g Glucides : 37,9 g]
[Sodium : 0,05 g]

Zucchinis sauce au yogourt

Pour **6** personnes • Préparation **15** min • Cuisson **9** min

Nutrition

Les zucchinis sont peu caloriques et vous fournissent des vitamines, minéraux et fibres. Cette recette est complète grâce à l'apport en calcium du yogourt. N'hésitez pas à l'accompagner de féculents.

- **1 kg** (**2 lb**) de zucchinis coupés en cubes de 2 cm (¾ po)
- **425 mL** (**1 ¾ tasse**) de farine tout usage
- **4** [cuillère] d'huile de tournesol

Sauce au yogourt :

- **175 mL** (**¾ de tasse**) de yogourt nature sans matière grasse
- **4** gousses d'ail hachées
- **2** [cuillère] aneth hachée
- Sel et poivre

1 Roule les cubes de zucchinis dans la farine et enlève l'excès en les tapotant.

2 Demande à maman de mettre à chauffer l'huile dans ActiFry 2 min., puis de rajouter les cubes de zucchinis assaisonnés.
Cuire 7 min.

3 Prépare la sauce en ajoutant l'ail et l'aneth au yogourt et mélange bien. Maman rajoute le sel et le poivre.

TEMPS DE L'ENFANCE

262 kcal

le sais-tu ?
Le zucchini est une courge cueillie très jeune, bien avant sa maturité.
On trouve dans la même famille le potiron, le pâtisson et le potimarron.
sauce yogourt

le sais-tu ?

La semoule est une sorte de farine granuleuse faite à partir de grains de blé dur. Elle est employée pour faire des gâteaux de semoule, des potages et des couscous. Elle sert à la fabrication des pâtes alimentaires.

Information nutritionnelle par portion
[Protéines : 6,8 g Lipides : 8,4 g Glucides : 37,7 g]
[Sodium : 0,02 g]

Nutrition

Ce dessert est une utile gourmandise, qui vous permet de compléter vos apports en glucides complexes et en calcium. De plus, les amandes vous fournissent des antioxydants et des acides gras essentiels.

Halva à la semoule

Pour **6** personnes • Préparation **15** min • Cuisson **25** min

- 400 mL (1 ⅔ tasse) de semoule
- 75 mL (⅓ de tasse) d'amandes mondées
- 1 d'huile d'olive
- 1 de beurre
- 1 d'eau (pour humidifier la semoule)
- 3 de sucre
- 250 mL (1 tasse) de lait écrémé + 125 mL (½ tasse) d'eau chaude
- ½ d'essence de vanille

1 Mélange la semoule, l'huile d'olive, l'eau et les amandes. Demande à maman de mettre à cuire la préparation dans ActiFry pendant 15 min.

2 Mélange la vanille et le sucre dans l'eau chaude, puis rajoute le lait. Verse la préparation sur le mélange semoule amandes. Laisse cuire 10 min.

3 À la fin de la cuisson, demande à maman de mettre le tout dans un saladier et de couvrir avec un torchon pendant 10 min. pour finir la cuisson de la semoule.

Conseil : Saupoudre de sucre au moment de servir.

Information nutritionnelle par portion
[Protéines : 0,8 g Lipides : 4,4 g Glucides : 33,6 g]
[Sodium : 0 g]

Nutrition

Une façon saine et gourmande de terminer un repas avec ce dessert qui correspond à deux portions de fruit. La particularité des pommes réside dans leur teneur en pectine, une fibre qui contribue à une bonne satiété.

Pommes à la cannelle

Pour **6** personnes • Préparation **20** min • Cuisson **25** min

- **6** pommes golden lavées et épluchées
- **125 mL (½ tasse)** d'abricots secs en petits morceaux
- **5 mL (1 cuill. à thé)** de cannelle moulue
- **2** de sucre granulé
- **2** d'huile de tournesol

1. Demande à maman de couper les pommes en quartiers, de les peler et de les mettre dans ActiFry avec l'huile. Cuisson 20 min.
2. Ajoute les abricots et laisse cuire encore 5 min., jusqu'à ce que les pommes soient tendres.
3. Mélange le sucre et la cannelle pour accompagner les pommes chaudes.

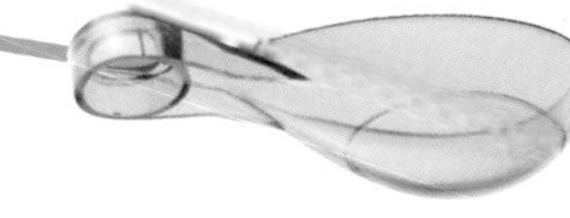

162 kcal

Connais-tu le dicton anglais ?
"Une pomme par jour éloigne le médecin".

Années d'adolescence

Temps des confidences et des échanges…

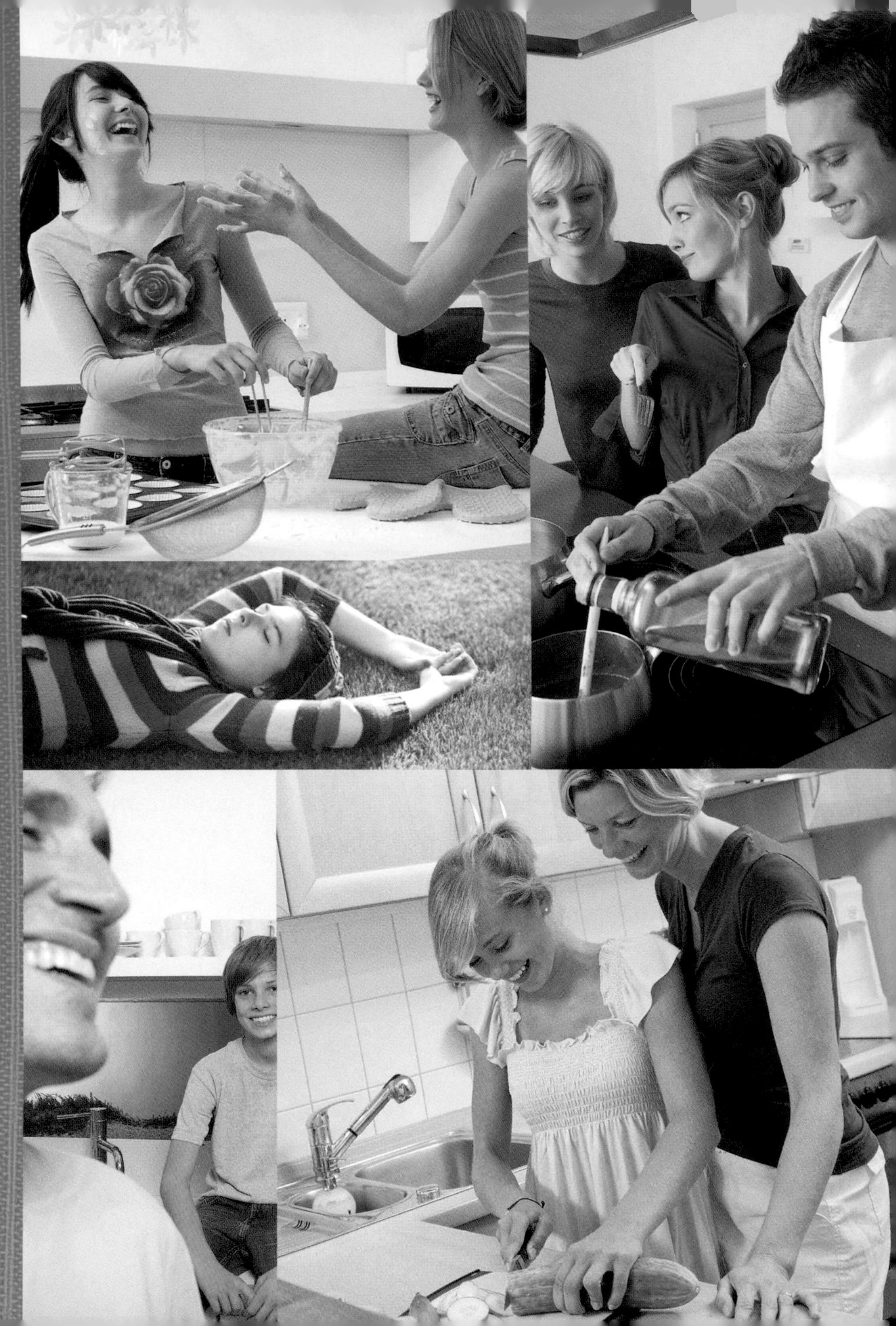

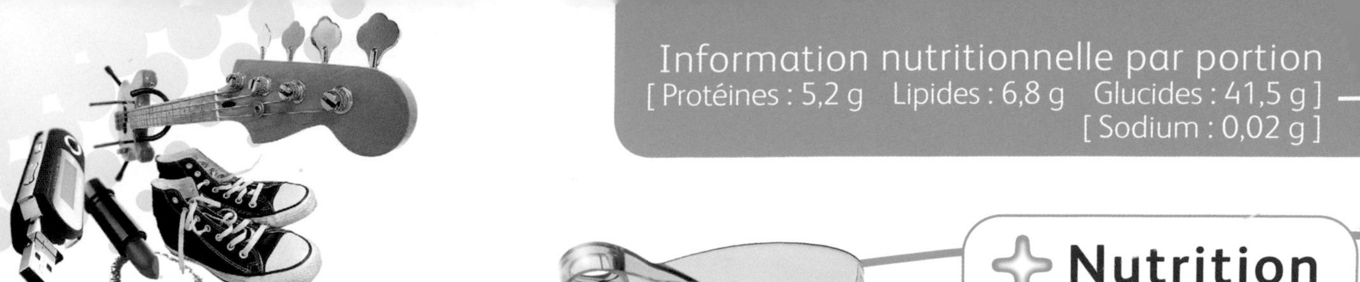

Information nutritionnelle par portion
[Protéines : 5,2 g Lipides : 6,8 g Glucides : 41,5 g]
[Sodium : 0,02 g]

Nutrition

Des frites moins grasses et plus savoureuses : voilà une bonne façon de convaincre les adolescents d'utiliser ActiFry.

Frites au curry

Pour **6** personnes • Préparation **15** min • Cuisson **45** min

1,5 kg (3 lb) de pommes de terre épluchées et lavées
1 d'huile végétale
2 d'huile de sésame
2 de curry

1. Coupez les pommes de terre en bâtonnets de 1 cm (½ po) d'épaisseur. Rincez-les abondamment, égouttez et séchez-les soigneusement.
2. Mélangez dans un bol l'huile végétale, l'huile de sésame et le curry.
3. Placez les frites dans ActiFry et versez le mélange uniformément sur les frites Laissez cuire pendant 45 min.

236 kcal

199 kcal

Information nutritionnelle par portion
[Protéines : 5,3 g Lipides : 2,5 g Glucides : 41,5 g]
[Sodium : 0,04 g]

Nutrition

Halte au grignotage! De quoi caler les fringales adolescentes avec un goût irrésistible.

Frites tex-mex

Pour **6** personnes • Préparation **15** min • Cuisson **55** min

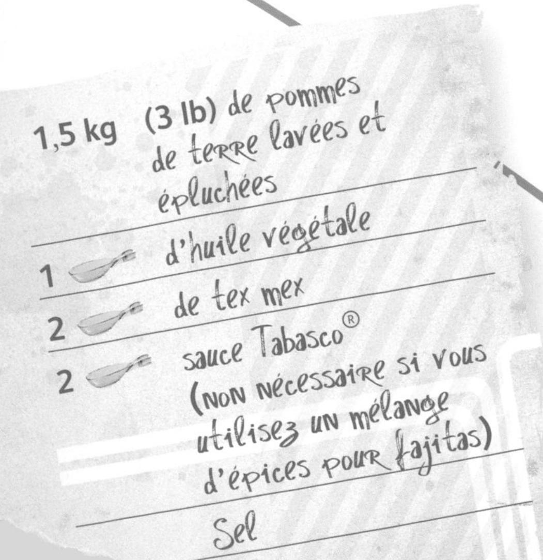

1. Coupez les pommes de terre en bâtonnets de 1 cm, rincez-les abondamment, égouttez et séchez-les soigneusement.

2. Mélangez dans un ramequin l'huile végétale et la poudre tex mex. Mettez les frites dans ActiFry et versez le mélange uniformément sur celles-ci. Laissez cuire 45 min.

3. Ouvrez ActiFry, salez et versez la sauce Tabasco® sur les frites puis prolongez la cuisson pendant 10 min.

Information nutritionnelle par portic
[Protéines : 35,9 g Lipides : 19 g Glucides : 7,1 g
[Sodium : 0,1 g]

Nutrition

La viande de bœuf est riche en fer et en vitamine B12 antianémique.

Boeuf à la Stroganoff

Pour **6** personnes • Préparation **10** min • Cuisson **10** min

1 kg (2 lb) de boeuf tendre
2 [cuillères] d'huile végétale
2 gros oignons émincés
2 [cuillères] de paprika
150 mL (⅔ de tasse) de crème de table à 18 %
Sel et poivre

1. Émincez la viande de bœuf et et mélangez-la avec le paprika.
2. Faites chauffer l'huile végétale et mettez à cuire les oignons pendant 4 min. Rajoutez le bœuf et laissez cuire 3-4 min.
3. Ajoutez la crème, faites bouillir 2 min., assaisonnez et servez.

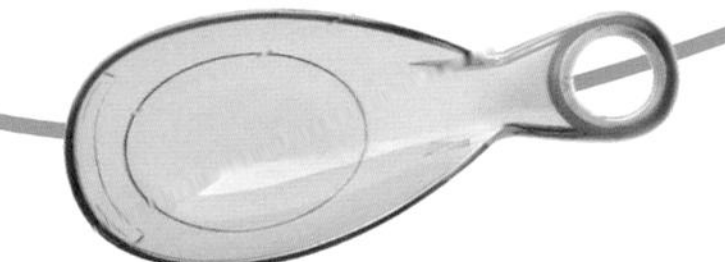

- 348 kcal

246 kcal

Information nutritionnelle par portion
[Protéines : 35,8 g Lipides : 9,1 g Glucides : 3,2 g]
[Sodium : 0,6 g]

Nutrition

Contrairement aux idées reçues, si on sait choisir le bon morceau, la viande de porc n'est pas particulièrement grasse. De plus, ses acides gras sont bien équilibrés.

Porc en bâtonnets

Pour **6** personnes • Préparation **15** min • Cuisson **25** min

- 1 kg (2 lb) de filet de porc coupés en bâtonnets
- 4 de sauce d'huîtres
- 3 de sauce soja
- 1 de sucre
- 1 d'huile de cuisson

1. Faites mariner le porc avec la sauce d'huîtres, la sauce soja, l'huile et le sucre pendant 1 h.
2. Dans ActiFry, mettez le porc avec sa marinade. Laissez cuire 25 min.

Conseil : Servez avec un riz frit.

Information nutritionnelle par portion
[Protéines : 30,4 g Lipides : 20,5 g Glucides : 12,2 g]
[Sodium : 0,4 g]

Nutrition

Le veau est une viande maigre qui fournit des protéines de bonne qualité ainsi que de la vitamine B12 aux propriétés antianémiques.
Des croquettes idéales pour toute la famille : en effet, les croquettes sont particulièrement appréciées par les enfants et les adolescents en raison de leur forme.

Croquettes de veau à la crème

Pour **6** personnes • Préparation **20** min • Cuisson **12** min

- 625 g (1 ¼ lb) de veau haché finement
- 150 mL (⅔ de tasse) de crème de table à 18 %
- 4 tranches de pain blanc
- 250 mL (1 tasse) de persil haché
- 175 mL (¾ de tasse) de parmesan râpé
- 2 oeufs entiers
- 3x1 d'huile d'olive
- Sel et poivre

1. Dans un saladier, mélangez le veau et le pain de mie ramolli au préalable dans la crème.
2. Ajoutez ensuite les œufs, le parmesan, le persil et assaisonnez. Confectionnez des croquettes en utilisant pour chacune environ 2 cuillerées à soupe (30 ml) du mélange.
3. Dans ActiFry, chauffez une cuillerée d'huile et faites cuire les croquettes sans les superposer pendant 8 min. Ajoutez ensuite ¼ de la crème restante et prolongez la cuisson de 4 min. Assaisonnez.

Conseil : Ne pas en mettre trop à la fois. Faire plusieurs tournées.

— 360 kcal

Nutrition

La viande de dinde contient une quantité importante de protéines de qualité et a l'avantage de présenter une faible teneur en matière grasse dont les acides gras, en majorité de type mono et poly-insaturés, contribuent au bon fonctionnement cardio-vasculaire.
Les poivrons sont une très bonne source de vitamines, en particulier la vitamine C.

Information nutritionnelle par portion
[Protéines : 39,6 g Lipides : 11,9 g Glucides : 25,3 g]
[Sodium : 0,1 g]

Filet de dinde
au trois poivrons

Pour **6** personnes • Préparation **20** min • Cuisson **35** min

- 1 kg (2 lb) de blancs de dinde en lanières 2,5 cm x 1 cm (1 po x ½ po)
- 6 poivrons épépinés (2 rouges, 2 verts, 2 jaunes)
- 2 oignons émincés
- 4 gousses d'ail hachées
- 3 cuillères d'huile d'olive
- 125 mL (½ tasse) verre de porto blanc
- 1 cuillère de vinaigre de cidre
- 125 mL (½ tasse) d'eau
- Sel et poivre

1. Faites cuire dans ActiFry pendant 15 min. les poivrons coupés en losanges de 2 cm (¾ po), les oignons et l'huile.
2. Rajoutez l'ail et faites cuire pendant 5 min. Assaisonnez.
3. Rajoutez les lanières de dinde, le porto blanc, l'eau, le vinaigre de cidre et laissez cuire environ 15 min.

Information nutritionnelle par portion
[Protéines : 51,7 g Lipides : 13,5 g Glucides : 0 g]
[Sodium : 0,2 g]

Nutrition

Les pilons de volaille consommés sans la peau fournissent des protéines de bonne qualité et contiennent peu de matière grasse. Ils sont très appréciés pour un dîner entre copains.

Pilons de volaille épicés

Pour **6** personnes • Préparation **5** min • Cuisson **25** min

- 1 kg (2 lb) de pilons de volaille sans la peau
- 2 de vinaigre de vin
- ½ de sauce Tabasco®
- 3 d'huile d'olive
- Sel

1. Dans un saladier, assaisonnez les pilons de volaille avec le vinaigre, le sel et la sauce Tabasco®. Laissez mariner une nuit.
2. Mettez l'huile à chauffer dans ActiFry et ajoutez les pilons avec la marinade. Laissez cuire 25 min.

Assaisonnements différents :

- Pour cette même recette, vous pouvez remplacer le vinaigre et et la sauce Tabasco® par de la moutarde de Dijon.
- Remplacez le vinaigre et et la sauce Tabasco® par du cumin et de l'huile de sésame.
- Ajoutez des graines de sésame 5 min. avant la fin de la cuisson.

342 kcal

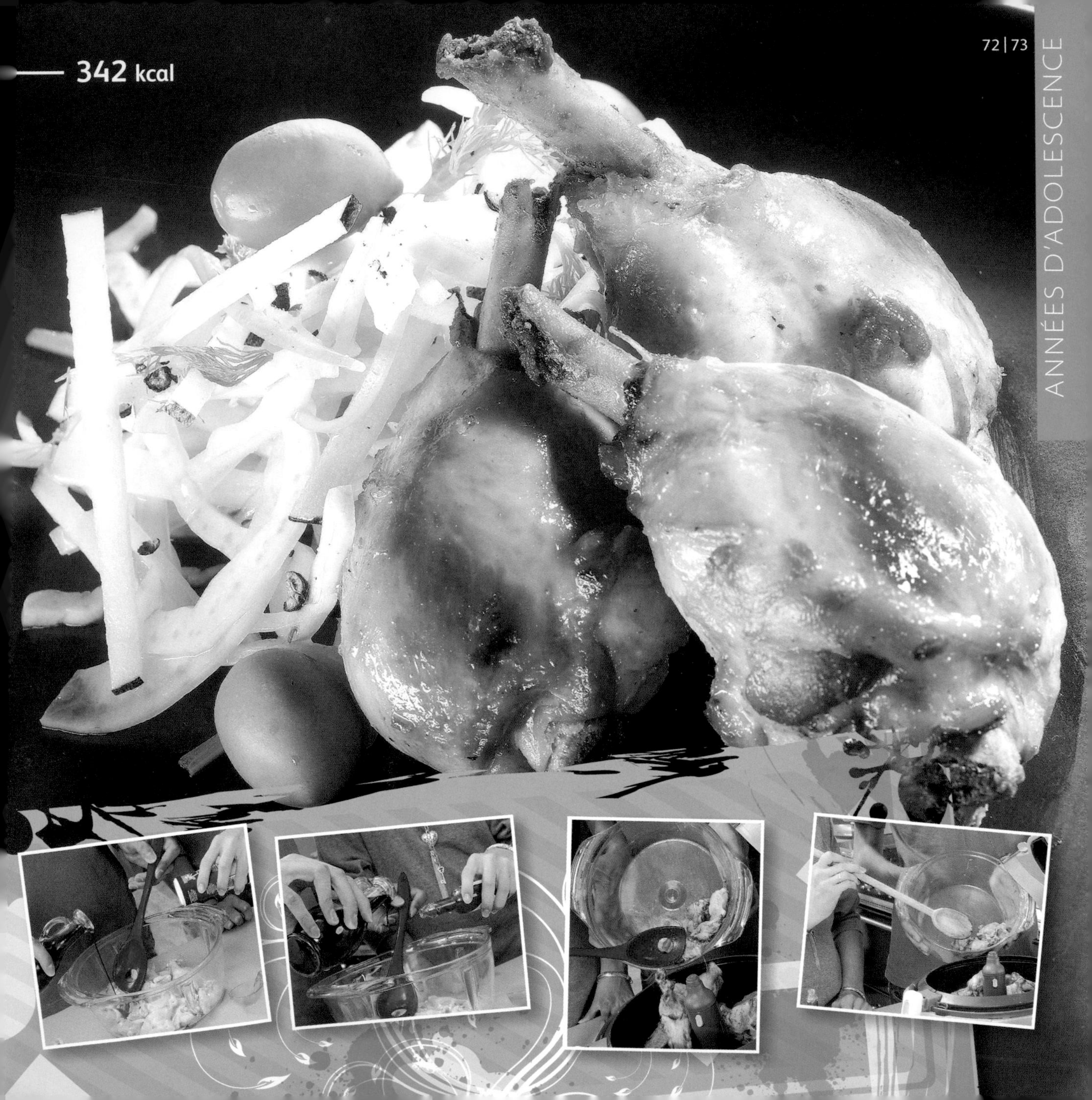

215 kcal
N.Y.

Information nutritionnelle par portion
[Protéines : 16,3 g Lipides : 13 g Glucides : 6,9 g]
[Sodium : 1,1 g]

Nutrition

Voici une bonne façon de redécouvrir le champignon, un légume unique pour son apport en protéines, en vitamines, en minéraux, et sa saveur boisée originale.

Poulet aux champignons et à l'estragon

Pour **6** personnes • Préparation **15** min • Cuisson **12** min

- 3 poitrines de poulet sans peau et coupées en dés
- 350 mL (1 ½ tasse) de champignons de Paris émincés
- 2 échalotes
- 75 mL (⅓ tasse) de vin blanc sec
- 250 mL (1 tasse) de crème sure
- 2 [cuillère] d'huile végétale
- 2 branches d'estragon effeuillées
- Sel et poivre

1 Faites chauffer l'huile dans ActiFry et mettez-y les morceaux de poulet assaisonnés. Laissez cuire 3 min. puis ajoutez les échalotes et les champignons de Paris et poursuivez la cuisson pendant 4 min.

2 Ajoutez le vin blanc et faites-le réduire pour y ajouter la crème. Faites bouillir 5 min. et ajoutez l'estragon. Rectifiez l'assaisonnement.

Information nutritionnelle par portion
[Protéines : 23 g Lipides : 8,7 g Glucides : 1,5 g]
[Sodium : 0 g]

Nutrition

Le fait de choisir du poulet sans peau et de le faire cuire dans ActiFry permet à cette recette d'être à la fois pauvre en matière grasse et riche en protéines de bonne qualité bonnes pour les muscles. L'utilisation de l'ail donne ici un petit plus : des propriétés digestives que vous pouvez renforcer en accompagnant ce plat d'un mélange de légumes et de céréales complètes.

Pilons de poulet à l'ail

Pour **6** personnes • Préparation **10** min • Cuisson **35** min

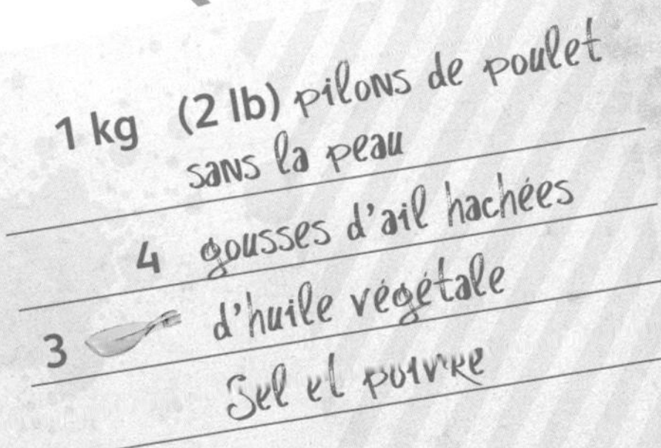

1 Déposez les pilons de poulet dans ActiFry avec l'huile et laissez-les cuire pendant 30 min.

2 Ajoutez l'ail haché et relancez en cuisson pendant 5 min. Salez et poivrez.

Conseil : Servez avec des pommes de terre au thym.

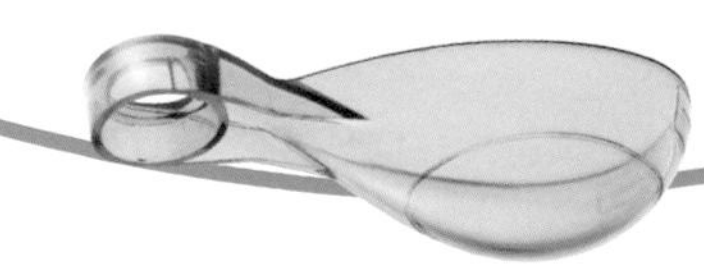

180 kcal

239 kcal

Nutrition

Les bénéfices nutritionnels des crevettes sont nombreux. Elles sont pauvres en matière grasse et riches en protéines de bonne qualité, indispensables au bon fonctionnement musculaire. De plus, elles sont riches en vitamines, en particulier la B12 qui contribue à la formation des globules rouges et la B3 qui libère de l'énergie pour les cellules de l'organisme. On y trouve également du zinc reconnu pour ses propriétés antioxydantes.

Information nutritionnelle par portion
[Protéines : 30,5 g Lipides : 5,8 g Glucides : 16,5 g]
[Sodium : 0,3 g]

Crevettes à la créole très piquantes

Pour **6** personnes • Préparation **15** min • Cuisson **23** min

- 24 grosses crevettes cuites décortiquées
- 2 oignons émincés
- 2 poivrons verts émincés
- 8 gousses d'ail hachées
- 3 [cuillère] d'épices cajuns
- 300 mL (1 ¼ tasse) purée de tomates
- 2 [cuillère] d'huile végétale
- Sel et poivre

1 Dans ActiFry, mettez l'huile à chauffer pendant 2 min. Ajoutez les oignons, les poivrons et l'ail. Laissez cuire pendant 6 min.

2 Ajoutez les épices cajuns, les crevettes et poursuivez la cuisson pendant 5 min.

3 Finissez en ajoutant la purée de tomate, laissez cuire pendant 10 min et assaisonnez à votre goût.

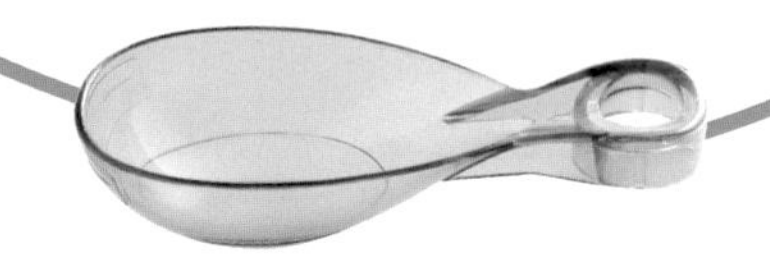

Information nutritionnelle par portion
[Protéines : 35,1 g Lipides : 11 g Glucides : 22,1 g]
[Sodium : 0,4 g]

Crevettes à la romaine

Pour **6** personnes • Préparation **30** min • Cuisson **20** min

875 g (1 ¾ lb) de crevettes décortiquées cuites
8 tomates épépinées et broyées (en conserve)
2 oignons coupés en rondelles
20 feuilles de basilic ciselé
4 d'huile d'olive
750 mL (3 tasses) de petit pois
Sel et poivre

1 Mettez les crevettes et les rondelles d'oignons dans ActiFry. Versez l'huile et faites cuire pendant 5 min.

2 Ajoutez les tomates broyées, les feuilles de basilic et les petits pois.
Assaisonnez et laissez cuire 15 min.
Rectifiez l'assaisonnement.

328 kcal

Nutrition

Cette recette vous fournit des protéines d'excellente qualité grâce aux crevettes qui ont en plus l'avantage de contenir peu de graisses. La cuisson dans ActiFry vous permet ici de profiter des qualités gustatives des crevettes, du basilic tout en ajoutant peu de matière grasse. De plus, les tomates fournissent du lycopène aux propriétés antioxydantes et les petits pois des glucides complexes qui contribuent à la satiété.

216 kcal

Information nutritionnelle par portion
[Protéines : 11,2 g Lipides : 9,3 g Glucides : 23,5 g]
[Sodium : 0,1 g]

Nutrition

Les œufs sont des aliments aux propriétés nutritionnelles très intéressantes : protéines de très bonne qualité indispensables au fonctionnement musculaire, vitamines A, E, zinc aux propriétés antioxydantes et vitamine D pour fixer le calcium sur les os. Les pommes de terre fournissent des glucides complexes excellents pour la satiété.

Tortillas d'oeufs brouillés à la ActiFry

Pour **6** personnes • Préparation **10** min • Cuisson **34** min

- 4 pommes de terre épluchées et lavées
- 1 oignon
- 8 oeufs
- 1 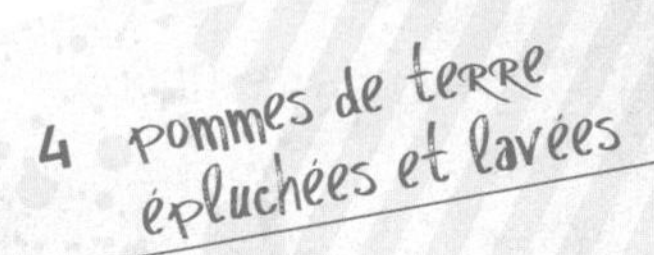 d'huile d'olive
- Sel et poivre

1. Coupez les pommes de terre en dés. Déposez-les dans ActiFry. Versez l'huile et faites cuire pendant 20 min.
2. Ajoutez l'oignon et laissez cuire 10 min. de plus.
3. Ajoutez les œufs battus et faites cuire 4 min. Assaisonnez.

Servez les tortillas d'oeufs brouillés dans un plat.

Information nutritionnelle par portion
[Protéines : 20,4 g Lipides : 10 g Glucides : 50,8 g]
[Sodium : 0,3 g]

Riz cantonais

Pour **6** personnes • Préparation **35** min • Cuisson **15-20** min

Nutrition

Avec ActiFry, vous pouvez préparer facilement un riz cantonais parfaitement équilibré. En effet, cette recette fournit à la fois des protéines de bonne qualité et des glucides complexes. N'hésitez pas à l'accompagner d'une salade verte assaisonnée d'huile de noix.

- 3 saucisses chinoises coupées en dés
- 18 crevettes cuites décortiquées
- 5 cuillères de petit pois
- 1,125 l (4 ½ tasses) de riz cuit
- 3 œufs battus
- 2 oignons hachés
- 1 cuillère d'huile de soja
- 2 cuillères d'eau
- Sel et poivre

1. Dans ActiFry, mettez les oignons avec l'huile et faites suer pendant 5 min.
2. Ajoutez les dés de saucisses et faites cuire pendant 5 min. Rajoutez les petits pois, les œufs et les crevettes. Poursuivez la cuisson pendant 5 min.
3. Ajoutez le riz cuit. Mettez un peu d'eau froide et laissez cuire 5 à 10 min. supplémentaires. Rectifiez l'assaisonnement et servez.

382 kcal

286 kcal

Conseil : Vous pouvez remplacer le grué de cacao par de la poudre de cacao amer ou du Nutella®.

Information nutritionnelle par portion

[Protéines : 6,5 g Lipides : 6,6 g Glucides : 31,6 g]
[Sodium : 0,01 g]

Nutrition

La feuille de brick contient très peu de matière grasse, c'est un excellent ingrédient pour réaliser des desserts feuilletés légers. Le grué de cacao contient une quantité intéressante de flavonoïdes aux propriétés antioxydantes.

Mini-pannequets de banane au grué de cacao à la ActiFry

Pour **6** personnes • Préparation **30** min • Cuisson **10** min

- 4 bananes pas trop mûres
- 2 [cuillères] de grué de cacao
- 9 feuilles de brick
- 2 œufs battus

Sauce :

- 125 mL (½ tasse) lait écrémé
- 100 g (3½ oz) de chocolat noir à 70%

1. Taillez les bananes en tranches de 1 cm (½ po) d'épaisseur. Coupez les feuilles de brick en 4.
2. Étalez un peu de grué de cacao au centre de la feuille, mettez un morceau de banane. Refermez en rabattant les 2 côtés opposés puis les deux autres cotés et badigeonnez avec l'œuf battu pour bien sceller les deux côtés. Déposez les pannequets dans ActiFry côté scellé vers le bas et faites cuire 10 min.
3. Pendant ce temps, faites chauffer le lait et incorporez le chocolat. Mixez pour homogénéiser la sauce.

Information nutritionnelle par portion
[Protéines : 2 g Lipides : 8 g Glucides : 33,1 g]
[Sodium : 0 g]

Nutrition

Ce dessert à base de pommes et de noisettes est une source intéressante de glucides complexes et d'acides gras essentiels.

Pommes Golden, noisettes et maïs soufflé

Pour **6** personnes • Préparation **20** min • Cuisson **30** min

- 6 pommes Golden
- 1 L (4 tasses) de maïs soufflé
- 75 mL (⅓ de tasse) de noisettes entières décortiquées
- 3 [cuillère] de caramel liquide

1 Épluchez et coupez les pommes en quartiers pour les épépiner puis taillez-les en dés de 1 cm (½ po) d'épaisseur.

2 Mettez les pommes dans ActiFry et versez le caramel uniformément sur celles-ci. Faites cuire 25 min.

3 Ajoutez les noisettes et le maïs soufflé puis prolongez la cuisson de 5 min.

199 kcal

Au cœur de la famille

Partage
et plaisir…

Information nutritionnelle par portion
[Protéines : 5,3 g   Lipides : 6,5 g   Glucides : 66,4 g]
[Sodium : 0,03 g]

Nutrition

Moins de matière grasse, mais plus de couleur et de saveur : voilà la preuve qu'un régime équilibré peut goûter bon !

Frites au paprika

Pour **6** personnes • Préparation **15** min • Cuisson **45** min

1,5 kg	(**3 lb**) de pommes de terre épluchées et lavées
1	d'huile végétale de qualité
2	d'huile de noisette
2	de paprika

1 Coupez les pommes de terre en bâtonnets de 1 cm (½ po) d'épaisseur. Rincez-les abondamment, égouttez et séchez-les soigneusement.

2 Mélangez dans un bol l'huile végétale, l'huile de noisette et le paprika.

3 Mettez les frites dans ActiFry et versez le mélange uniformément dessus. Laissez cuire 45 min.

256 kcal

425 kcal

Information nutritionnelle par portion
[Protéines : 39,5 g   Lipides : 26 g   Glucides : 4,8 g]
[Sodium : 0,1 g]

Nutrition

Les lipides de l'agneau, ajoutés à ceux de l'huile de noisette, sont en majorité des acides gras favorisant le bon fonctionnement du système cardio-vasculaire. La richesse en lipides de ce plat en fait une recette à réserver pour des occasions particulières.

Agneau rissolé aux noisettes

Pour **6** personnes • Préparation **15** min • Cuisson **20** min

- **1 kg** **(2 lb)** d'agneau (épaule ou selle) découpé en lamelles de 2,5 cm x 1 cm (1 po x ½ po)
- **2** [cuillère] d'huile de noisette
- **250 mL** **(1 tasse)** de noisettes torréfiées
- **125 mL** **(½ tasse)** d'eau
- **150 mL** **(⅔ de tasse)** de vin blanc sec
- Sel et poivre

Sauce :

- **2** œufs
- **6** citrons en jus

1. Mettez l'agneau dans ActiFry, versez l'huile et faites cuire pendant 7 min.
2. Salez, poivrez, ajoutez le verre d'eau et le verre de vin blanc. Laissez cuire 13 min.
3. Ajoutez les noisettes que vous aurez préalablement grillées et pelées.

Sauce citron :

1. Battez les œufs et incorporez le jus des citrons en fouettant.
2. Ajoutez un peu de jus de cuisson en fouettant énergiquement.

Information nutritionnelle par portion
[Protéines : 35,5 g Lipides : 15,1 g Glucides : 16,3 g]
[Sodium : 0,2 g]

Tajine d'agneau aux citrons confits et olives noires

Pour **6** personnes • Préparation **25** min • Cuisson **25-30** min

- **1 kg** (**2 lb**) d'épaule d'agneau coupée en cubes de 30 g (1 oz)
- **30 g** (**1 oz**) de gingembre émincé
- **75 mL** (**⅓ de tasse**) d'olives noires dénoyautées
- **3** citrons confits
- **3** gousses d'ail émincées
- **1** bouquet de coriandre ciselé
- **125 mL** (**½ tasse**) de persil hâché
- **2** de gingembre en poudre
- **4** stigmates de safran
- **2** de fécule de maïs
- **150 mL** (**⅔ de tasse**) de vin blanc
- **2** d'huile d'olive
- Sel et poivre

1 Émincez les zestes de citrons finement après avoir enlevé la pulpe. Délayez la fécule de maïs, le safran dans 150 ml (⅔ de tasse) d'eau et le vin.

2 Mettez l'huile, le gingembre, l'ail et l'oignon dans ActiFry et faites cuire 5 min. Ajoutez la viande et prolongez la cuisson de 10 min.

3 Ajoutez le reste des ingrédients et laissez cuire encore 10 à 15 min. selon votre goût. Assaisonnez.

Conseil : Saupoudrez les herbes au moment de servir.

369 kcal

Nutrition

Il est important de souligner que l'agneau, même s'il fait partie des viandes grasses, présente des avantages sur le plan nutritionnel : acides gras oméga 9 qui contribuent à rééquilibrer le profil lipidique, fer, zinc, phosphore, et vitamines du groupe B. C'est pourquoi, pour profiter de ces bénéfices, nous vous recommandons de choisir pour cette recette un morceau maigre comme l'épaule dégraissée. Accompagné de légumes cuits à la vapeur, ce plat hautement parfumé peut parfaitement s'intégrer à une alimentation équilibrée.

362 kcal

Information nutritionnelle par portion
[Protéines : 33,4 g Lipides : 12,3 g Glucides : 30,3 g]
[Sodium : 0,9 g]

Nutrition

Cette recette allie parfaitement protéines animales dans le bœuf et protéines végétales dans les haricots rouges ; ces dernières sont nécessaires au bon fonctionnement musculaire. Ce repas vous fournit également des fibres qui contribuent à une bonne digestion ainsi que du lycopène aux propriétés antioxydantes que l'on trouve dans les tomates.

Bœuf aux haricots

Pour **6** personnes • Préparation **10** min • Cuisson **14** min

- **750 g** (**1 ½ lb**) de steak maigre
- **1** [cuillère] d'huile d'olive
- **1** gros oignon émincé
- **625 mL** (**2 ½ tasses**) de tomates en dés avec leur jus (en conserve)
- **300 mL** (**1 ¼ tasse**) de bœuf à faible teneur en sodium
- **1** [cuillère] de thym en fleur
- **750 mL** (**3 tasses**) de haricots rouges (en conserve) rincés et égouttés
- Sel et poivre

1 Dégraissez la viande et coupez-la en fines lanières. Mettez l'huile et l'oignon dans ActiFry et faites cuire 5 min. Ajoutez la viande et continuez la cuisson pendant 5 min.

2 Ajoutez les tomates et leur jus, le bouillon, le thym et les haricots et faites cuire pendant 4 min. Assaisonnez avec du poivre noir.

Conseil : Servez avec des tortillas ou des nachos.

Information nutritionnelle par portion
[Protéines : 22,4 g Lipides : 12,2 g Glucides : 6,2 g]
[Sodium : 0,2 g]

Accompagnée de pâtes, de riz ou de polenta, cette sauce riche en protéines et en légumes constitue un repas complet, équilibré du point de vue nutritionnel, qui peut se terminer avec un produit laitier et un fruit.

Sauce à la bolognaise

Pour **6** personnes • Préparation **10** min • Cuisson **50** min

- **625 g** (**1 ¼ lb**) de bœuf haché extra maigre
- **1** oignon ciselé
- **125 mL** (**½ tasse**) de vin rouge
- **500 g** (**1 lb**) de tomates pelées
- **3** d'huile d'olive
- Sel et poivre

1 Faites chauffer l'huile dans ActiFry, mettez l'oignon à cuire 5 min. Rajoutez la viande hachée, assaisonnez et laissez cuire 10 min.

2 Mouillez avec le vin rouge et poursuivez la cuisson pendant 5 min.

3 Ajoutez les tomates pelées et passées au mélangeur et laissez cuire pendant 30 min.

Conseil : Servez avec des macaronis.

237 kcal

389 kcal

Information nutritionnelle par portion
[Protéines : 34,3 g Lipides : 17,4 g Glucides : 11,9 g]
[Sodium : 0,07 g]

Nutrition

Le lapin est une viande particulièrement intéressante du point de vue nutritionnel : pauvre en matière grasse, elle fournit du fer et de la vitamine B12 anti-anémique, mais aussi des protéines utiles pour le bon fonctionnement musculaire.

Lapin au citron et au thym

Pour **6** personnes • Préparation **20** min • Cuisson **25** min

- **1 kg** (**2 lb**) de râble de lapin coupé en petits morceaux
- 4 d'huile d'olive
- 2 gros oignons émincés
- 4 citrons en jus
- **250 mL** (**1 tasse**) vin blanc sec
- **125 mL** (**½ tasse**) d'eau
- **125 mL** (**½ tasse**) de persil
- 2 branches de thym frais
- Sel et poivre blanc

1 Faites cuire l'oignon dans 2 cuillerées d'huile d'olive pendant 5 min.

2 Ajoutez ensuite les morceaux de lapin avec le reste de l'huile d'olive, le thym, le vin blanc sec, le jus de citrons et 1 verre d'eau. Assaisonnez et laissez cuire 20 min.

3 En fin de cuisson, saupoudrez de persil haché et de fleur de thym.

Conseil : Servez avec des pommes de terre à la vapeur.

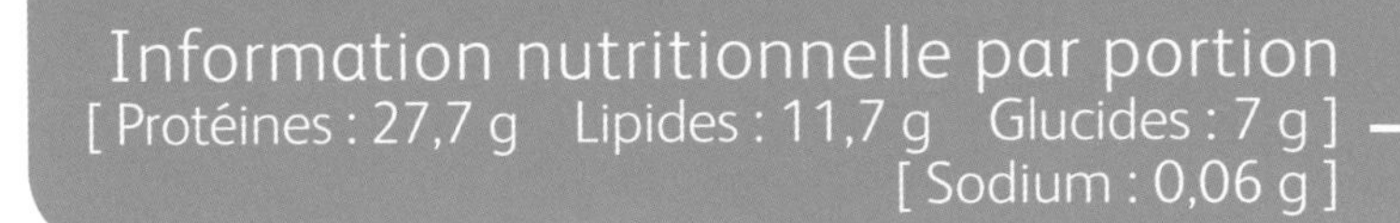

Information nutritionnelle par portion
[Protéines : 27,7 g   Lipides : 11,7 g   Glucides : 7 g]
[Sodium : 0,06 g]

Nutrition

Le lapin est une viande particulièrement intéressante du point de vue nutritionnel : pauvre en matière grasse, elle apporte du fer et de la vitamine B12 anti-anémique, mais aussi des protéines utiles pour le bon fonctionnement musculaire.

Lapin au piment d'Espelette

Pour **6** personnes • Préparation **15** min • Cuisson **45** min

- **1** lapin de 1,5 kg (3 lb) coupé en petits morceaux
- **1** poivron rouge
- **150 mL** (**⅔ de tasse**) de vin blanc
- **2** gousses d'ail hachées
- **1** oignon émincé
- **2** d'huile d'olive
- **½** de piment d'Espelette
- Sel et poivre

1. Faites chauffer l'huile dans ActiFry avant de mettre le lapin assaisonné et laissez cuire pendant 5 min.
2. Ajoutez le poivron, l'ail, l'oignon et le piment d'Espelette. Poursuivez la cuisson pendant 15 min.
3. Mouillez avec le vin blanc et faites cuire pendant encore 25 min. Rectifiez l'assaisonnement.

266 kcal

323 kcal

Information nutritionnelle par portion
[Protéines : 35,4 g Lipides : 13,6 g Glucides : 3,8 g]
[Sodium : 0,09 g]

Nutrition

Cette recette est riche en protéines de bonne qualité. De plus, l'huile d'olive contient des acides gras mono-insaturés qui contribuent au bon fonctionnement cardio-vasculaire.

Filet de porc à la mode d'Alentejo

Pour **6** personnes • Préparation **15** min • Cuisson **20** min

- **1 kg** (**2 lb**) de filet de porc coupé en cubes
- **1** oignon émincé
- **300 mL** (**1 ¼ tasse**) de vin blanc
- **3** [cuillère] d'huile d'olive
- Paprika à volonté
- Sel et poivre

1 Mettez l'huile et l'oignon dans ActiFry et laissez dorer pendant 5 min.

2 Ajoutez la viande, le sel, le poivre et du paprika. Arrosez avec le vin blanc et laissez cuire pendant 15 min.

Conseil : Servez avec des frites cuites dans ActiFry.

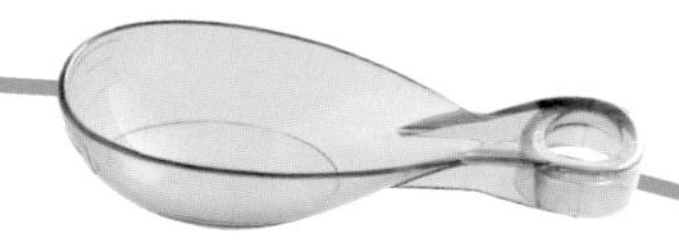

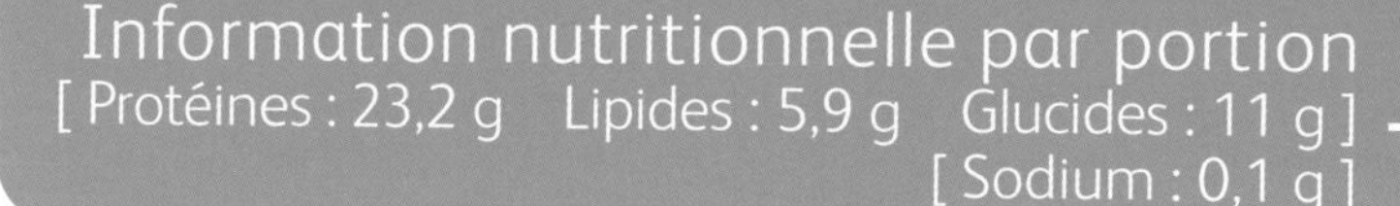

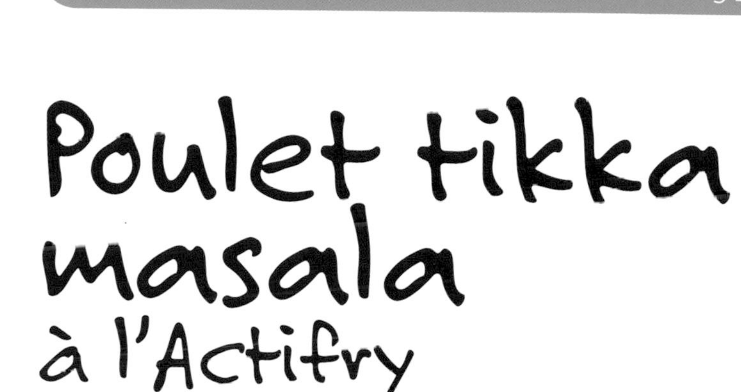

pour **6** personnes • Préparation **15** min • Cuisson **30** min

500 g	(**1 lb**) de poitrines de poulet désossées, coupées en morceaux de 2 cm
100 g	de pâte de cari Tikka Masala
2 pots	(**format de 150 g**) de yogourt naturel faible en gras
1	d'huile végétale
1	gros oignon haché fin
390 g	(**1 boîte de conserve**) de tomates hachées de première qualité
150 mL	(**⅔ de tasse**) d'eau
½	cuillerée à thé de sucre
2	cuillerées à thé de jus de citron frais
1	bouquet de feuilles de coriandre hachées

1 Dans un grand bol, mélangez la pâte Tikka masala avec 3 cuillerées à soupe de yogourt. Ajoutez le poulet en brassant le tout afin de bien recouvrir le poulet. Laissez-le mariner au réfrigérateur pendant au moins 2 heures ou pendant la nuit, si vous disposez de ce temps.

2 Faites chauffer l'huile dans ActiFry pendant 2 minutes, ajoutez l'oignon et laissez cuire pendant 5 minutes. Ajoutez le poulet mariné et laissez cuire le tout pendant encore 10 minutes.

3 Ajoutez les tomates hachées et l'eau. Laissez cuire encore 10 minutes. Ajoutez le yogourt, le sucre et le jus de citron. Brassez le mélange à l'aide d'une cuillère en bois et laissez-le cuire pendant encore 5 minutes. Servez le poulet chaud en le saupoudrant de coriandre hachée, accompagné d'un riz basmati ou de pain naan.

Conseil : accompagnez de riz blanc.

— 191 kcal

Nutrition

Habituellement, le poulet masala évoque un plat gras préparé avec du ghee (beurre) et de la crème. Cette version à plus faible teneur en gras requiert plutôt de l'huile végétale à la place du beurre ainsi que du yogourt faible en gras, ce qui rend ce plat plus sain.

226 kcal

Information nutritionnelle par portion
[Protéines : 28 g Lipides : 7 g Glucides : 14 g]
[Sodium : 0,1 g]

Nutrition

Le terme Kebab fait généralement penser à un plat très riche en matière grasse. Dans cette version de la recette, le choix du filet de veau ainsi que la faible quantité d'huile utilisée en font un plat parfaitement équilibré et léger.

Kebab ActiFrit

Pour **6** personnes • Préparation **15** min • Cuisson **27** min

- **750 g** (**1 ½ lb**) de filet de veau
- **2** citrons en jus
- **2** de piment rouge en poudre
- **500 mL** (**2 tasses**) de coulis de tomates
- **2** gousses d'ail hachées
- **1** oignon ciselé
- **1** d'huile d'olive
- **75 mL** (**⅓ de tasse**) de cumin en poudre
- Sel

1 Coupez le filet de veau en cubes et mélangez avec le citron, le cumin et le piment rouge.

2 Faites cuire l'ail et l'oignon avec l'huile pendant 5 min. Ajoutez ensuite les morceaux de veau et laissez cuire 15 min de plus.

3 Ajoutez le coulis de tomate et faites cuire encore 7 min. Servez chaud.

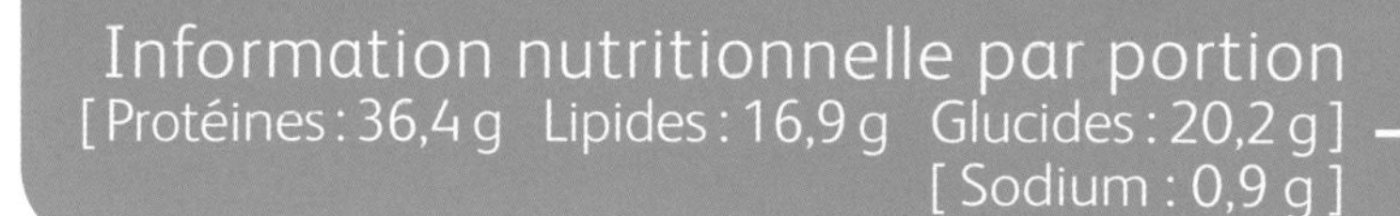

Information nutritionnelle par portion
[Protéines : 36,4 g Lipides : 16,9 g Glucides : 20,2 g]
[Sodium : 0,9 g]

Nutrition

Cette recette allie protéines de bonne qualité du veau pour les muscles et acides gras essentiels pour le bon fonctionnement cardio-vasculaire.

Émincés de veau aux olives

Pour **6** personnes • Préparation **10** min • Cuisson **30** min

1 kg	**(2 lb)** de filet de veau coupé en lanières de 1 cm x 2,5 cm (½ po x 1 po)
150 mL	**(⅔ de tasse)** de farine tout usage
750 mL	**(3 tasses)** d'oignons blancs hachés
4	d'huile d'olive
500 mL	**(2 tasses)** de bouillon de poulet à faible teneur en sodium
1	poignée de persil ciselé
20	olives
	Sel et poivre

1 Faites revenir les oignons 5 min. dans ActiFry avec l'huile.

2 Ajoutez le fond de veau et les olives et faites cuire 5 min.

3 Mélangez dans un saladier le veau, la farine et assaisonnez. Versez le tout dans ActiFry et faites cuire 20 min.

Conseil : Servez avec des pâtes fraîches.

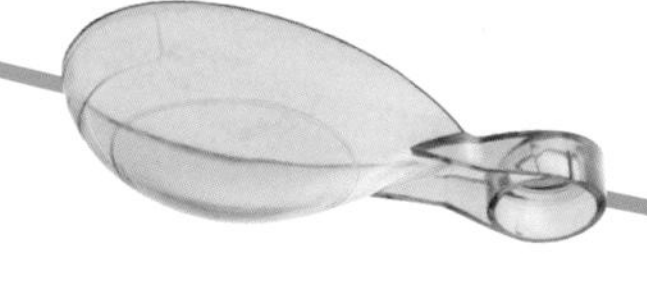

381 kcal

251 kcal

Information nutritionnelle par portion
[Protéines : 31,4 g Lipides : 7,8 g Glucides : 15 g]
[Sodium : 2,5 g]

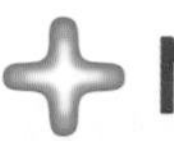

Nutrition

La viande de volailles contient de « bonnes graisses », car ces dernières sont essentiellement mono et poly insaturées et contribuent au bon fonctionnement du système cardio-vasculaire. De plus, l'ananas compte bon nombre de minéraux et de vitamines.

Poulet à l'ananas

Pour **6** personnes • Préparation **15** min • Cuisson **18** min

- **1 kg** (**2 lb**) de poitrines de poulet coupées en fines lanières (½ po x 1 po)
- **500 mL** (**2 tasses**) d'ananas coupé en cubes
- 3 (cuillère) de sauce soja
- 3 (cuillère) de jus d'ananas
- 1,5 (cuillère) de fécule + 1 cuil. à soupe (15 mL)
- 1 (cuillère) de gingembre
- 1 (cuillère) de curry doux
- 3 (cuillère) d'huile végétale
- **250 mL** (**1 tasse**) d'eau
- Sel et poivre

1 Dans un saladier, enrobez les lanières de poulet avec un mélange de fécule, de sel et de poivre. Mettez-les dans ActiFry, versez l'huile végétale et laissez cuire 8 min.

2 Arrêtez ActiFry, ajoutez le gingembre, le curry et l'ananas, mélangez et laissez macérer 5 min. Puis allongez avec la sauce soja et l'eau. Rajoutez 1 cuillère à soupe de fécule délayée dans le jus de l'ananas.

3 Faites cuire de nouveau pendant 5 min.

Conseil : Servez avec un riz basmati parfumé ou un riz sauvage.

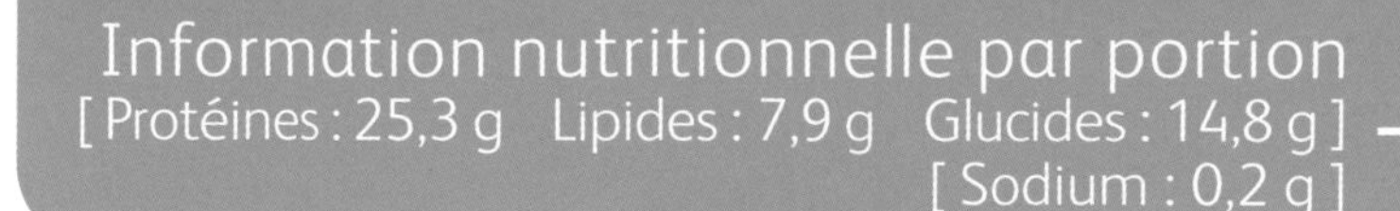

Poulet
aux petits pois et carottes

Nutrition

Le poulet est une viande à faible teneur en matière grasse qui contient des protéines de bonne qualité. Ces dernières sont complétées par les protéines végétales que contiennent les petits pois.

Pour **6** personnes • Préparation **15** min • Cuisson **20** min

- **625 g** (**1 ¼ lb**) de poulet sans la peau, émincé
- **500 mL** (**2 tasses**) de petits pois surgelés
- **500 mL** (**2 tasses**) de carottes surgelées
- **1** oignon ciselé
- **2** pâte de tomate diluée dans 250 mL (1 tasse) d'eau
- **2** d'huile d'olive
- Sel et poivre

1 Dans ActiFry, mettez l'huile et le poulet à cuire pendant 5 min.
Ajoutez l'oignon et faites cuire de nouveau pendant 5 min.

2 Ajoutez les petits pois, les carottes et la sauce tomate. Laissez cuire 10 min. de plus.
Salez, poivrez.

— 230 kcal

304 kcal

Information nutritionnelle par portion
[Protéines : 35,1 g Lipides : 13,1 g Glucides : 11 g]
[Sodium : 0,25 g]

Nutrition

Les gambas sont très peu caloriques et contiennent essentiellement des protéines de bonne qualité indispensables au bon fonctionnement musculaire et des vitamines du groupe B.

Gambas à la Provençale

Pour **6** personnes • Préparation **20** min • Cuisson **15** min

1 kg (**2 lb**) de gambas crues décortiquées
2 oignons émincés
6 gousses d'ail hachées
125 mL (**½ tasse**) de persil haché
5 [cuillère] d'huile d'olive
2 citrons
Sel et poivre

1 Faites mariner. les gambas avec l'ail, l'oignon, le persil et l'huile pendant 15 min. Assaisonnez votre marinade.

2 Mettez les gambas et la marinade dans ActiFry pendant 15 min. Quand les gambas prennent une belle couleur orangée, vous pouvez les déguster.

3 Servez avec des quartiers de citrons.

Conseil : Des rinces-doigts peuvent être utiles : petit bol d'eau tiède avec du citron.

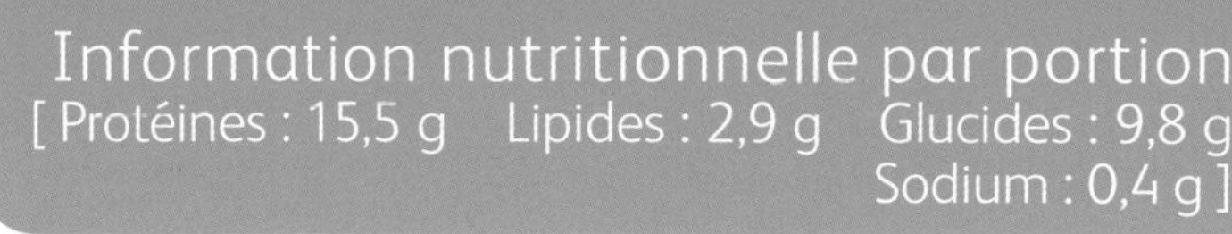

Information nutritionnelle par portion
[Protéines : 15,5 g Lipides : 2,9 g Glucides : 9,8 g
Sodium : 0,4 g]

Moules marinières aux tomates-cerises et basilic

Pour **6** personnes • Préparation **20** min • Cuisson **29** min

Nutrition

La moule est une excellente source de protéines et contient des acides gras oméga 3 protecteurs du système cardio-vasculaire. De plus, elle est une mine de nutriments essentiels : phosphore, fer, zinc, sélénium, cuivre, vitamines B1, B2, B12, B3, B9. La tomate contient du lycopène, un pigment rouge aux propriétés antioxydantes. Accompagnée d'une petite portion de riz et d'un filet d'huile d'olive, cette recette donnera un plat parfaitement équilibré.

3 kg	(**6 lb**) de moules
625 g	(**1 ¼ lb**) de tomates cerises
1	oignon ciselé
300 mL	(**1 ¼ tasse**) de vin blanc
3	gousses d'ail
1	bouquet de basilic
	Sel et poivre

1 Nettoyez les moules et les tomates-cerises. La cuisson des moules se fera en 3 fois

2 Dans ActiFry, faites cuire les oignons les tomates cerises, l'ail et le vin blanc pendant 8 min. Ajoutez les moules, le sel et le poivre et cuire 7 min.

3 Retirez la première fournée de moules et ajoutez le basilic sur le dessus. Dégustez-les, tout en relançant les autres fournées.

— **166** kcal

144 kcal

Information nutritionnelle par portion
[Protéines : 4,7 g Lipides : 6,7 g Glucides : 15,5 g]
[Sodium : 0,02 g]

Nutrition

Cette recette est idéale en accompagnement de rôtis de viande ou de poissons. Elle est riche en légumes mais surtout en vitamines et minéraux. Ces atouts sont complétés par le bon apport en antioxydants de l'huile d'olive.

Sauté méditerranéen de légumes

Pour **6** personnes • Préparation **10** min • Cuisson **30** min

- **2** zucchinis
- **1 l** (**4 tasses**) de champignons
- **1** aubergine
- **1** poivron rouge
- **½** poivron vert
- **150 mL** (**⅔ de tasse**) de vin blanc
- **3** de gousses d'ail broyées
- Persil (quelques branches)
- **3** d'huile d'olive
- Sel et poivre

1 Coupez les zucchinis et l'aubergine en cubes. Émincez les champignons. Coupez les poivrons en fines lanières.

2 Mettez l'aubergine, les zucchinis, les poivrons et les champignons dans ActiFry. Versez l'huile et faites cuire pendant 15 min.

3 Broyez l'ail et le persil. Ajoutez le vin blanc. Assaisonnez et prolongez la cuisson de 15 min.

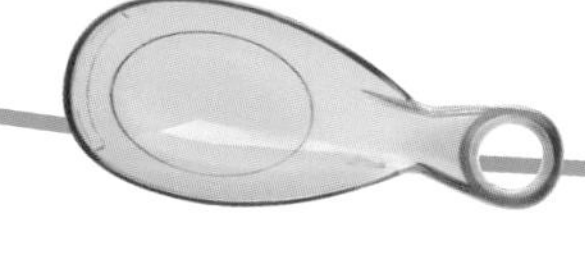

Information nutritionnelle par portion
[Protéines : 23,8 g Lipides : 18,2 g Glucides : 63,3 g]
[Sodium : 1,9 g]

Nutrition

Les glucides complexes (à absorption lente) du riz entraînent une libération progressive d'énergie évitant ainsi «le petit creux» et donc les grignotages entre les repas. La quantité de parmesan, contribue à combler vos besoins calciques pour la solidité osseuse. La teneur en protéines végétales intéressantes du riz spécial risotto et du parmesan fait de cette recette un plat idéal à consommer au souper.

Risotto aux tomates séchées et oignons verts

Pour **6** personnes • Préparation **10** min • Cuisson **30** min

375 mL	(**1 ½ tasse**) de riz spécial rosotto ou arborio
45 mL	(**3 c. à soupe**) de beurre
575 mL	(**2 ⅓ tasses**) parmesan
800 mL	(**3 ¼ tasses**) de bouillon de légumes
18	tomates séchées dans l'huile, coupées en dés
8	oignons verts émincés
	Sel et poivre

1 Faites chauffer le beurre 3 min. dans ActiFry et mettez le riz en ajoutant 2 min. de cuisson.

2 Ajoutez le bouillon et faites cuire le tout pendant 25 minutes.

3 En fin de cuisson, ajoutez le parmesan, les tomates et les oignons verts, puis assaisonnez.

500 kcal

497 kcal

Information nutritionnelle par portion
[Protéines : 32,4 g Lipides : 16,5 g Glucides : 44,9 g]
[Sodium : 1,3 g]

Nutrition

Ce risotto est un plat équilibré et complet. Il fournit à la fois des protéines de bonne qualité pour les muscles ainsi que de l'iode et des glucides complexes pour assurer la satiété. Il sera idéalement accompagné d'une entrée de crudités et d'un fruit pour compléter les apports en vitamines et fibres.

Risotto au curry

Pour **6** personnes • Préparation **15** min • Cuisson **32** min

- **375 g** (**1 ½ tasse**) de riz cru
- **125 mL** (**½ tasse**) d'oignons hâchés
- **36** crevettes décortiquées cuites
- **2 mL** (**½ c. à soupe**) de curry
- **30 mL** (**7 c. à soupe**) de beurre
- **250 mL** (**1 tasse**) de vin blanc
- **125 mL** (**½ tasse**) de coriandre hâché
- **575 mL** (**2 ⅓ tasses**) de parmesan râpé
- **750 mL** (**3 tasses**) de bouillon de poulet à faible teneur en sodium

1. Faites fondre le beurre dans ActiFry, ajoutez l'oignon et laissez cuire 5 min. Ajoutez le riz, le curry et laissez rissoler 2 min. puis versez le vin blanc et laissez réduire à sec.
2. Versez le bouillon et laissez cuire pendant 25 minutes. Ajoutez ensuite le parmesan, les crevettes et la coriandre. Assaisonnez au goût.
3. En fin de cuisson, le risotto doit être onctueux.

Information nutritionnelle par portion
[Protéines : 24,6 g Lipides : 14,7 g Glucides : 32,8 g]
[Sodium : 0,2 g]

Tofu ActiFrit à l'espagnole

Pour **6** personnes • Préparation **15** min • Cuisson **35** min

750 g	(**1 ½ lb**) de tofu nature ferme
1	gros poivrons (en dés)
1	grosse tomate hachée
500 mL	(**2 tasses**) de riz basmati cuit
40 g	(**1 ½ oz**) de chorizo en fines tranches
75 mL	(**⅓ de tasse**) d'olives noires dénoyautées
1 (cuillère)	de pâte ou de purée de tomate
1	gros oignon ciselé
	Sel et poivre

1. Dans ActiFry, mettez à cuire l'oignon et les poivrons pendant 10 min.
2. Faites cuire le tout pendant 10 minutes, puis rajoutez la pâte de tomate, les tomates hachées et les olives. Prolongez la cuisson de 5 min.
3. Égouttez le tofu, taillez-le en dés de 1 cm (½ po) et rajoutez-le dans ActiFry, cuisson 5 min.
4. Incorporez le riz et laissez cuire 5 min. de plus. Assaisonnez à votre goût.

— 345 kcal

Nutrition

Contrairement à la plupart des protéines végétales, les protéines de soja que l'on trouve dans le tofu ont une excellente valeur biologique, c'est-à-dire qu'elles contiennent tous les acides aminés dont notre corps a besoin : aucun risque de carence avec cette paëlla végétarienne parfaitement équilibrée! Les poivrons et la tomate contiennent de la vitamine C, des flavonoïdes et des caroténoïdes aux propriétés antioxydantes. Enfin, le riz basmati contient des glucides complexes qui permettent d'augmenter l'effet de satiété et de tenir jusqu'au repas suivant sans fringale.

178 kcal

Information nutritionnelle par portion
[Protéines : 5,5 g Lipides : 13,8 g Glucides : 9,9 g]
[Sodium : 0,1 g]

Nutrition

Voici une façon originale de redécouvrir les haricots verts. Vous bénéficiez ainsi de leurs nombreux atouts nutritionnels tout en dégustant de nouvelles saveurs : vitamine A aux propriétés antioxydantes, C pour la vitalité et B9 au rôle important pour l'immunité. Sans oublier les vertus digestives de la sauge.

Haricots verts étuvés à la sauge fraîche et amandes

Pour **6** personnes • Préparation **5** min • Cuisson **20** min

1 kg	(**2 lb**) de haricots verts équeutés
75 mL	(**⅓ de tasse**) d'amandes entières ou effilées
50 mL	(**¼ de tasse**) de sauge fraîche hachée
150 mL	(**⅔ de tasse**) à fouetter à 35 %
1 (cuillère)	d'huile
150 mL	(**⅔ de tasse**) d'eau
	Sel et poivre

1. Versez l'huile dans ActiFry et faites cuire les haricots environ 10 min. avec l'eau et la sauge.
2. Ajoutez ensuite les amandes et la crème. Laissez cuire 10 min. de plus. Salez et poivrez à votre goût.

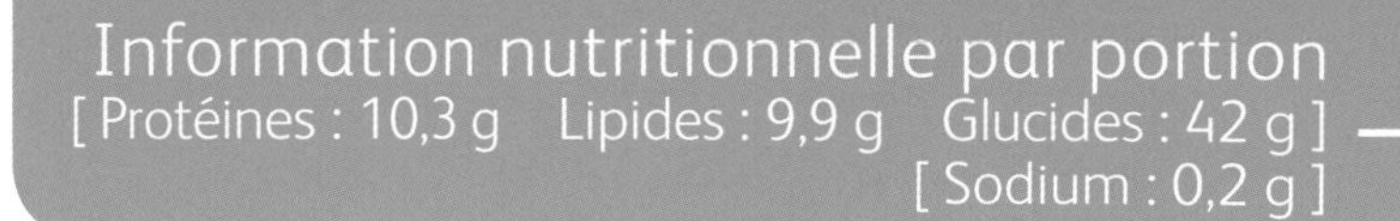

Information nutritionnelle par portion
[Protéines : 10,3 g Lipides : 9,9 g Glucides : 42 g]
[Sodium : 0,2 g]

Légumes à l'italienne

Pour **6** personnes • Préparation **20** min • Cuisson **40** min

Nutrition

Ce plat de légumes à l'italienne illustre parfaitement la cuisine méditerranéenne. Il offre un repas complet et une des cinq portions de fruits et légumes recommandées. La quantité de fibres et de vitamines est particulièrement intéressante.

2	aubergines coupées en petit cubes
875 mL	(**3 ½ tasses**) de haricots verts miniatures équeutés et hachés
3	poivrons jaunes (grillés, pelés, épépinés) en lanières
1	petit chou romanesco (en fleurettes)
2	oignons émincés
2	gousses d'ail écrasées
250 mL	(**1 tasse**) d'olives noires dénoyautées et coupées en morceaux
3	d'huile d'olive
250 mL	(**1 tasse**) de basilic en feuilles
	Sel et poivre

1 Mettez les oignons, les aubergines, les poivrons et l'huile dans ActiFry. Faites cuire pendant 10 min.

2 Ajoutez les haricots, le chou et l'ail écrasé. Assaisonnez et ajoutez 375 ml (1 ½ tasse) d'eau. Continuez la cuisson 30 min.

3 Incorporez les olives et le basilic. Salez et poivrez.

Conseil : Servez avec des tagliatelles fraîches.

283 kcal

299 kcal

Nutrition

La patate douce est peu représentée dans notre culture culinaire, et c'est bien dommage!
Comme la betterave et le potiron, elle contient de nombreux pigments antioxydants qui contribuent à la prévention du vieillissement cellulaire.
Ces légumes renferment également d'importantes quantités de fibres alimentaires qui contribuent à une bonne digestion intestinal et à la régulation du taux de cholestérol.
L'huile d'olive, quant à elle, fournit de la vitamine E antioxydante ainsi que des acides gras oméga 9 protecteurs du système cardio-vasculaire.

Information nutritionnelle par portion
[Protéines : 6,5 g   Lipides : 6,5 g   Glucides : 57,7 g]
[Sodium : 0,1 g]

Terrine de légumes râpés avec citron et ciboulette

Pour **6** personnes • Préparation **30** min • Cuisson **30** min pour chaque légume

750 g	(**1 ½ lb**) de pommes de terre râpées
750 g	(**1 ½ lb**) de patates douces râpées
625 g	(**1 ¼ lb**) de citrouille pelée et râpée
250 g	(**½ lb**) de betteraves cuites râpées
1	citron en jus
125 mL	(**½ tasse**) de ciboulette fraîche ciselée
3	d'huile d'olive
	Sel et poivre

1 Ajoutez une cuillerée d'huile aux pommes de terre râpées, une à la citrouille râpée et une aux patates douces. Assaisonnez chaque légume. Faites cuire les pommes de terre râpées dans ActiFry pendant 30 minutes.

2 Enlevez les pommes de terre et râpées et faites cuire les patates douces râpées. Terminez par la cuisson du râpé de citrouille.

3 Montez des étages de chaque légume dans un moule à gâteau et terminez par la ciboulette et le jus de citron. Couvrez d'une pellicule transparente et laissez reposer pendant 12 heures au réfrigérateur en mettant un poids dessus.

Information nutritionnelle par portion
[Protéines : 3,3 g   Lipides : 8,6 g   Glucides : 17,4 g]
[Sodium : 0,01 g]

Nutrition

Cette recette qui évoque le soleil est une mine de vitamines, en particulier la vitamine C pour la vitalité, et d'antioxidants comme le lycopène et de fibres. L'huile d'olive contient des acides gras mono-insaturés qui contribuent au bon fonctionnement du système cardio-vasculaire.

Ratatouille

Pour **6** personnes • Préparation **25** min • Cuisson **31** min

- **1** oignon ciselé
- **3** grosses tomates en dés
- **2** aubergines en dés de 2 cm (3/4 po)
- **2** zucchinis en dés de 2 cm (3/4 po)
- **2** poivrons verts en dés de 2 cm (3/4 po)
- **2** poivrons rouges en dés de 2 cm (3/4 po)
- **5** gousses d'ail hachées
- **4** (cuillère) d'huile d'olive
- Sel et fleur de thym

1 Mettez l'huile dans ActiFry et laissez chauffer pendant 1 min. Faites cuire l'oignon et les poivrons pendant 5 min.

2 Ajoutez les aubergines, les zucchinis et l'ail. Continuez la cuisson pendant 15 min.

3 Pour terminer, ajoutez les tomates et faites cuire pendant 10 minutes. Assaisonnez votre ratatouille et mettez un peu de fleur de thym.

— 147 kcal

77 kcal

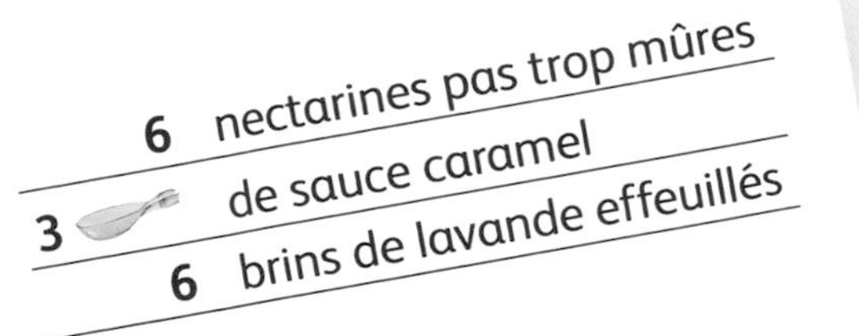

Information nutritionnelle par portion
[Protéines : 1,4 g   Lipides : 0,4 g   Glucides : 18,7 g]
[Sodium : 0 g]

Nutrition

Les nectarines possèdent des propriétés désaltérantes grâce à leur teneur importante en eau. De plus, elles sont une source intéressante de vitamine C pour la vitalité et une bonne immunité et sont très riches en provitamine A pour la protection de la peau.

Nectarines à la lavande

Pour **6** personnes • Préparation **15** min • Cuisson **7** min

- **6** nectarines pas trop mûres
- **3** de sauce caramel
- **6** brins de lavande effeuillés

1 Dans une eau bouillante, trempez les nectarines 30 secondes et refroidissez-les aussitôt. Pelez-les et coupez-les en quartiers.

2 Faites chauffer le caramel dans ActiFry pendant 4 min. Ajoutez les quartiers de nectarines et prolongez la cuisson 3 min.

3 Saupoudrez de lavande en fin de cuisson.

Conseil : Servez chaud avec une glace à la vanille ou des amandes.

Information nutritionnelle par portion
[Protéines : 2,1 g   Lipides : 8 g   Glucides : 15,6 g]
[Sodium : 0 g]

Nutrition

Ce délicieux dessert est peu calorique tout en étant gourmand.

Abricots aux amandes

Pour **6** personnes • Préparation **5** min • Cuisson **5** min

12	abricots charnus et pas trop mûrs
50 mL	(**¼ de tasse**) d'amandes entières ou effilées
1 (cuillère)	de jus de citron
45 mL	(**3 c. à soupe**) de beurre
4 (cuillères)	de sucre cristallisé
90 mL	(**6 c. à soupe**) d'eau

1 Mettez dans ActiFry le beurre et le sucre cristallisé, mouillez avec l'eau. Chauffez le mélange jusqu'à obtenir un jus sirupeux. Ajoutez le jus de citron.

2 Une fois le mélange bouillant, placez les abricots, partie coupée vers le bas. Laissez cuire 2 à 3 min., puis retournez-les et laissez de nouveau cuire 1 à 2 min. en rajoutant les amandes.

Conseil : Pour les plus gourmands, rajoutez une goutte d'eau de vie d'abricots du Valais en fin de cuisson.

— 135 kcal

249 kcal

Nutrition

Une note de gourmandise grâce à ce crumble gourmand qui satisfait vos besoins en fibres pour une bonne digestion, en glucides complexes pour la satiété mais également en bétacarotène aux propriétés antioxydantes.

Information nutritionnelle par portion
[Protéines : 26 g Lipides : 9,3 g Glucides : 6 g]
[Sodium : 0 g]

Crumble pomme-mangue

Pour **6** personnes • Préparation **15** min • Cuisson **15** + **20** min

5	pommes épluchées et coupées en dés
1	mangue mûre coupée en dés
½ (cuillère)	de miel
¼ (cuillère)	de gingembre frais haché finement
½ (cuillère)	de menthe fraîche hachée
1 (cuillère)	de poudre de noisettes (optionnel)
	Coulis de fruits rouges non-sucré (surgelé)
Pour le crumble :	
150 mL	(**⅔ de tasse**) de farine tout usage
50 mL	(**¼ de tasse**) de beurre à température ambiante
5 (cuillère)	de sucre cristallisé

1 Mettez les pommes et le miel dans ActiFry et faites cuire pendant 15 min.

2 Ajoutez la mangue, le gingembre et la menthe et laissez cuire 5 min.

3 Servez dans un verre : mettez du coulis de fruits rouges dans le fond du verre, placez les fruits par-dessus et saupoudrez un peu de Crumble sur les fruits.

Pour le crumble :

1 Mélangez la farine et le sucre dans un bol, ajoutez le beurre et mélangez du bout des doigts (la pâte doit rester émiettée).

2 Mettez la préparation dans ActiFry et faites cuire 15 min. jusqu'à ce que le Crumble soit blond doré. Gardez dans un bol.

Conseil : si la mangue n'est pas tout à fait mûre, faites-la cuire en même temps que les pommes.

Information nutritionnelle par portion
[Protéines : 1,3 g Lipides : 4,3 g Glucides : 42,7 g]
[Sodium : 0 g]

Nutrition

Ce dessert vous permet de compléter vos apports en vitamines et minéraux de la journée.

Pommes et bananes ActiFrites à la lime et coriandre

Pour **6** personnes • Préparation **20** min • Cuisson **15** min

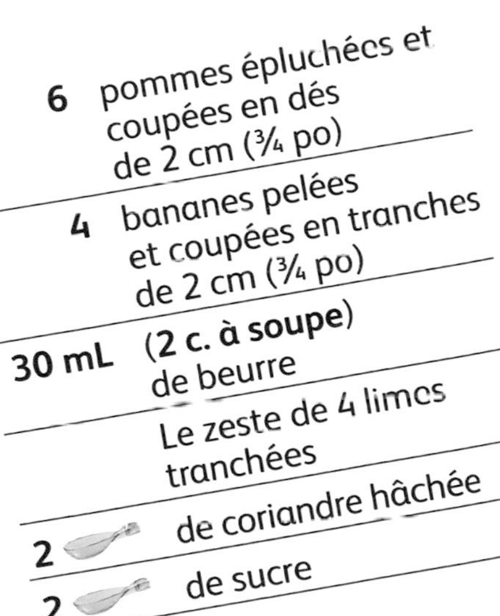

6	pommes épluchées et coupées en dés de 2 cm (3/4 po)
4	bananes pelées et coupées en tranches de 2 cm (3/4 po)
30 mL	**(2 c. à soupe)** de beurre
	Le zeste de 4 limes tranchées
2 (cuillère)	de coriandre hâchée
2 (cuillère)	de sucre

1 Mélangez les pommes et le sucre dans un saladier. Déposez ensuite le mélange dans ActiFry après avoir fait fondre le beurre et faites cuire pendant 10 min.

2 Ajoutez les bananes et prolongez la cuisson de 5 min.

3 Ajoutez les zestes des limes et la coriandre en fin de cuisson.

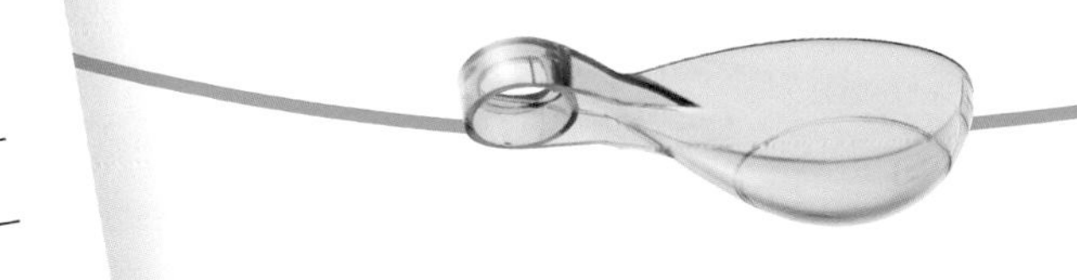

197 kcal

289 kcal

Information nutritionnelle par portion
[Protéines : 2,8 g Lipides : 12 g Glucides : 48 g]
[Sodium : 0 g]

Nutrition

Ce dessert, mélange de fruits frais et fruits secs, contient des vitamines, minéraux et fibres ainsi que des acides gras essentiels qui contribuent au bon fonctionnement du système cardio-vasculaire.

Quartiers de pommes et de poires aux noix

Pour **6** personnes • Préparation **15** min • Cuisson **20** min

- **3** pommes Granny Smith épluchées et coupées en quartiers
- **3** poires épluchées et coupées en quartiers
- **250 mL** (**1 tasse**) de noix
- **2** d'huile de noix
- **2** de jus de pomme
- **1** de cannelle en poudre
- **75 mL** (**⅓ de tasse**) de raisins secs

1 Faites mariner les fruits dans l'huile et la cannelle pendant 30 min.

2 Mettez les fruits avec la marinade à cuire dans ActiFry pendant 10 min. Ajoutez le jus de pomme, les noix, les raisins secs et laissez cuire 10 min. de plus.

Information nutritionnelle par portion
[Protéines : 2 g   Lipides : 4,7 g   Glucides : 33,5 g]
[Sodium : 0 g]

Nutrition

Ce dessert, très frais, fournit des vitamines en quantités intéressantes, A et C en particulier, mais également des fibres.

Soupe de pêches
menthe fraîche et grenadine

Pour **6** personnes • Préparation **25** min • Cuisson **20** min

12	pêches blanches
5 ml	(**1 c. à thé**) d'eau de fleur d'oranger
125 mL	(**½ tasse**) de sirop de grenadine
2 (cuillères)	d'huile d'olive
1 (cuillère)	de Ras el hanout ou de cumin en poudre
	Quelques feuilles de menthe fraîche

1 Trempez les pêches pendant 20 secondes dans de l'eau bouillante puis aussitôt dans de l'eau glacée. Épluchez-les et coupez-les en quartiers.

2 Mettez dans ActiFry l'eau de fleur d'oranger, la grenadine, l'huile et l'épice choisie.

3 Ajoutez les quartiers de pêches et faites cuire 20 min.

Conseil : Servez bien frais, accompagné de feuilles de menthe et d'une boule de sorbet.

— 173 kcal

174 kcal

Information nutritionnelle par portion
[Protéines : 1 g   Lipides : 0,4 g   Glucides : 46,3 g]
[Sodium : 0 g]

Ananas et mangues rôties

Pour **6** personnes • Préparation **15** min • Cuisson **20** min

Nutrition

Ce dessert aux ananas et à la mangue contient des fibres qui sont bonnes pour la digestion, des vitamines comme la vitamine C pour la vitalité et la vitamine A pour la beauté de la peau. La teneur en vitamine C de l'ananas est d'autant plus intéressante que cette vitamine fragile qui s'oxyde à la lumière est protégée par la peau épaisse du fruit jusqu'à ce qu'il soit ouvert.

- 1 ananas
- 2 mangues pelées
- Le jus de 2 citrons
- 4 (cuillerées) de miel
- 1 pincée de cannelle en poudre

1 Découpez la couronne et la partie inférieure de l'ananas. Enlevez l'écorce, coupez-le en 8 et retirez le cœur puis taillez-le en petit dés de 1cm (½ po). Coupez les mangues de la même grosseur que l'ananas.

2 Mettez les morceaux de mangue dans ActiFry et versez 2 cuillerées de miel. Laissez cuire 10 min.

3 Ajoutez l'ananas avec le reste du miel, le jus de citron et la cannelle. Laissez cuire 10 min. de plus.

Conseil : Servez tiède avec une boule de glace à la vanille.

Temps de

Pommes de terre

	TYPE	QUANTITE	AJOUT	TEMPS DE CUISSON
Frites taille standard 10 mm x 10 mm	Fraîches	1500 g (3 ⅓ lb)	1 c. d'huile	45 min
		1000 g (2 ¼ lb)	¾ c. d'huile	38 min
		750 g (1 lb 11 oz)	½ c. d'huile	32 min
		500 g (1 lb 2 oz)	¼ c. d'huile	26 min
		250 g (9 oz)	⅛ c. d'huile	22 min
Frites MacCain tradition	Surgelées	1200 g (2 ⅔ lb)	sans	40 min
		750 g (1 lb 11 oz)	sans	27 min

c. = cuillère ActiFry

Viandes - Volailles

	TYPE	QUANTITE	AJOUT	TEMPS DE CUISSON
Pépites de poulet	Fraîches	1200 g (2 ⅔ lb)	Sans	20 min
	Surgelées	1200 g (2 ⅔ lb)	Sans	20 min
Pilons de poulet	Frais	9	Sans	30 min
Cuisses de poulet	Fraîches	3	Sans	35 min
Poitrines de poulet	Fraîches	9 poitrines (environ 1200 g / 2 ⅔ lb)	Sans	25 min
Nems	Frais	12 petits	1 c. d'huile	12 min
Paupiettes de veau	Fraîches	9	1 c. d'huile	25 min
Côtes de porc	Fraîches	6	1 c. d'huile	20 min
Filet de porc	Frais	9	1 c. d'huile	15 min
Râbles de lapin	Frais	9	1 c. d'huile	20 min
Viande hachée	Fraîche	900 g (2 lb)	1 c. d'huile	15min
	Surgelée	600 g (1 ⅓ lb)	1 c. d'huile	15 min
Boulettes de viande	Surgelées	1200 g (2 ⅔ lb)	1 c. d'huile	20 min

cuisson

Poissons - Crustacés

	TYPE	QUANTITE	AJOUT	TEMPS DE CUISSON
Beignets de calamars	Surgelés	500 g (1 lb 2 oz)	Sans	14 min
Crevettes	Cuites	600 g (1 ⅓ lb)	Sans	8 min
Gambas	Surgelées	450 g (1 lb)	Sans	10 min

Légumes

	TYPE	QUANTITE	AJOUT	TEMPS DE CUISSON
Courgettes	Fraîches en lamelles	1,2 kg (2 ⅔ lb)	1 c. d'huile + 150 mL (5 fl oz) d'eau	30 min
Poivrons	Frais en lamelles	1 kg (2 ¼ lb)	1 c. d'huile + 250 mL (9 fl oz) d'eau	25 min
Champignons	Frais en quartiers	1 kg (2 ¼ lb)	1 c. d'huile	20 min
Tomates	Fraîches en quartiers	1 kg (2 ¼ lb)	1 c. d'huile	20 min
Oignons	Frais en rondelles	750 g (1 lb 11 oz)	1 c. d'huile	30 min

Préparations surgelées

	TYPE	QUANTITE	AJOUT	TEMPS DE CUISSON
Ratatouille	Surgelée	1000 g (2 ¼ lb)	Sans	32 min
Poêlée pâtes et poisson	Surgelée	1000 g (2 ¼ lb)	Sans	22 min
Poêlée paysanne	Surgelée	1000 g (2 ¼ lb)	Sans	30 min
Poêlée savoyarde	Surgelée	1000 g (2 ¼ lb)	Sans	25 min
Pâtes à la carbonara	Surgelées	1000 g (2 ¼ lb)	Sans	20 min
Paëlla	Surgelée	1000 g (2 ¼ lb)	Sans	20 min
Riz cantonais	Surgelé	1000 g (2 ¼ lb)	Sans	20 min
Chili con carne	Surgelé	1000 g (2 ¼ lb)	Sans	15 min

Desserts

	TYPE	QUANTITE	AJOUT	TEMPS DE CUISSON
Bananes	En rondelles	700 g (1 lb 9 oz) (7 bananes)	1 c. d'huile + 1 c. de sucre roux	6 min
	En papillotes	3 bananes	Sans	20 min
Cerises	Entières	1500 g (3 ⅓ lb)	1 c. d'huile + 2 c. de sucre	15 min
Fraises	Coupées en quatre	1500 g (3 ⅓ lb)	2 c. de sucre	7 min
Pommes	Coupées en deux	5	1 c. d'huile + 2 c. de sucre	12 min
Poires	Coupées en morceaux	1500 g (3 ⅓ lb)	2 c. de sucre	12 min
Ananas	Coupé en morceaux	2	2 c. de sucre	17 min

Recettes par

ENFANTS

ADOS

chapitre

FAMILLE

Index par

Fruits

Légumes

Œufs

Poissons

ingrédient

Pomme de terre

Riz

Semoule

Viande

Agneau

Bœuf

Dinde

Lapin

Porc

Veau

Volaille

ma recette

ma recette

Remerciements :
Docteur Johannes M. Peil
Docteur Christian Recchia
Docteur Marianna Trifonova
Kim Arrey
Nathalie Hutter Lardeau
Glenis Noble
Association Canadienne du Diabète

SA SEB - 21261 SELONGEY CEDEX - RCS B 302 412 226

Adaptation des recettes :
David Le Comte

Rédaction nutritionnelle :
Atlantic Santé

Conception et réalisation graphique :
JPM & Associés

Crédits photos :
Inmagine - Getty image - Matton - Fotolia -
Image & Associés - Studio Rougereau

Fabrication :
Typocentre

NUTRITION
GOURMANDE™

NUTRITIOUS
& DELICIOUS™

Acknowledgements:
Doctor Johannes M. Peil
Doctor Christian Recchia
Doctor Marianna Trifonova
Kim Arrey
Nathalie Hutter Lardeau
Glenis Noble
Canadian Diabetes Association

SA SEB - 21261 SELONGEY CEDEX - RCS B 302 412 226

Recipe adaptation:
David Le Comte

Nutritional content:
Atlantic Santé

Graphic design and layout:
JPM & Associés

Photo credits:
Inmagine - Getty image - Matton - Fotolia
Image & Associés - Studio Rougereau

Production:
Typocentre

Translation:
Pro-fusion